A Survey of Contemporary Issues

After finishing L7 and L8, students apply their knowledge to the new world around us. Advanced course on Islam with topics related to contemporary issues, including philosophy, atheism, gender interaction, feminism, new social contracts (same-sex, etc.), alternate theories on the world and human life, etc.

Ghamidi Center
of Islamic Learning
www.ghamidi.org   AN INITIATIVE OF AL-MAWRID US.

Publisher: Ghamidi Center of Islamic Learning - Al-Mawrid US
ISBN: 978-1-966600-33-6

Address: 3620 N Josey Ln, Suite 230 Carrollton, TX 75007
Website: www.ghamidicenter.com
Email: info@ghamidi.org

Chapter 1

Introduction to the Course

Introduction

- The tragic incident of 9/11, recent violence and turmoil in many Muslim lands, and not-so-thoughtful responses of Muslim intellectuals on modern-day issues have raised many questions in the minds of sincere Muslims.

- In a traditional society, tradition is accorded centrality, but in today's world, reason plays a central role. The rational mind of this modern age is asking:

  - *"If Islam is the religion of peace, then why is terrorism associated with Islam?*
  - *"If the Quran gives equal status to men and women, then why are Muslim women oppressed in many Muslim societies worldwide, and is the husband allowed to beat his wife?"*
  - *"How can a religion of mercy not allow a Muslim to pet a dog?"*
  - *"If God has created all human beings, then why are people of the LGBTQ community not accepted in a Muslim society?*
  - *"If science explains everything, what do I need religion for?"*
  - *"Can Islam respond to the challenges faced in the contemporary world?"*
  - *"Is Islam even compatible with the modern world?"*

- This course is designed to answer these and similar questions raised in modern minds, in light of the Quran, Sunnah, and the rich, long tradition of Islamic scholarship.

- Contrary to common belief, Islam has provided fundamental guiding principles for various aspects of the Muslim individual and society, leaving the details of practical application to the human faculty of jurisprudence, so that different societies can apply the guiding principles of *Shariah* according to time and place.

Objectives

- The main objective of this course is to survey contemporary issues and understand Islam's position on them.

- The foundational knowledge built in Levels 7 and 8 will be applied in this level first to appreciate the problem and then to understand Islam's approach to addressing it.

- Along the way, this course will also attempt to clarify some misunderstandings about Islam and present the correct perspective on these topics.

Topics covered in this course

- ▶ Quick Introduction to Islam and Islamic Sciences
- ▶ Our relationship with non-Muslims
- ▶ Islam and Terrorism
- ▶ Democracy or Caliphate?
- ▶ The Punishment for Apostasy
- ▶ The Punishment for Blasphemy
- ▶ Homosexuality and LGBTQ interactions
- ▶ Women's Rights, Abortion and Misconceptions
- ▶ Slavery and Sex with Slaves
- ▶ Polygamy, Marriage and Halalah
- ▶ Music and Other Forms of Art
- ▶ Keeping Dogs
- ▶ Tattoos, Magic, and Witchcraft
- ▶ Pornography and Masturbation
- ▶ Modern Science, Big Bang, and Evolution
- ▶ Atheism
- ▶ Cloning, Organ Donation, Sex-change Operations, Cosmetic Surgery, Assisted Suicide
- ▶ Hijab
- ▶ Dating and Falling in Love

Is Islam compatible with the modern world?

- Islam is not one of many religions – it is the only religion of God.
- Islamic Shariah is based on the very nature in which human beings are created.
- Islam does not provide a complete 'system' in every domain of life, but rather offers fundamental guiding principles related to Shariah.
- Details are left to the human faculty of jurisprudence so that different societies can apply those principles according to time and place.
- It provides answers to questions that transcend time and place.

If I am a creation, who is my Creator then?   How did this universe and I begin?

What is death?   Is this life the beginning or the end?

What happens after death?   Why is this universe so perfectly designed?

Where is my strong moral sense coming from?

How can I explain love, hatred, sacrifice, and motherhood?

The Main Problems

- The debate about Islam's compatibility with the modern world stemmed from two main problems:

Problem #1	The Quran and the Prophet have been presented as the "problem solver" for **all** the issues that human societies face.
Problem #2	Today's religious scholarship is wrongfully trying to present religion **in comparison to** modern philosophies and physical sciences.

- Religion serves a unique purpose in Muslims' lives. Its main realm is our death and life after death. With life after death as the center and focus, it gives us certain principles, in the form of Shariah, to morally purify ourselves, individually and collectively.
- With those moral guidelines in place (four corners), we are free to run the affairs of this world.

Islamic Resources

Join Ask Ghamidi
A community-driven discussion portal to ask, answer, share, and learn

https://www.ghamidi.org/app/

Meezan Lectures – English
By Dr. Shehzad Saleem

https://youtube.com/playlist?list=PL3yXG2ufxd6USiyYQVHtzpXAnMvXC4-C9&si=er-IHTj1ZelulyO2

Annotated linguistic resource on Quran with Arabic grammar, syntax, and morphology for each word

https://corpus.quran.com/

Islam – A Comprehensive Introduction
Meezan translation by Dr. Shehzad Saleem

https://archive.org/ (Use Search option)

Quran Translation and Commentary by Javed Ahmed Ghamidi
https://www.javedahmedghamidi.org/#!/quran-home

Hadith Resources
https://ahadith.co.uk/
https://sunnah.com/

Important Notes

- You are required to attend all classes unless you have a valid reason to skip.
- Please send a note (or ask your parents) to your teacher on Google Classroom if you will skip a session.
- Attendance will be taken at the beginning of every class. Arriving in class 5 minutes after the start will be considered tardy.
- Three (3) tardies will be counted as one absence.
- Attendance will be counted toward your final assessment.
- Every student will be assessed via:
    - Participation in the class
    - Multiple Quizzes
    - Assignments
    - Semester Exam
    - End-of-Year Exam

Chapter 2

Islam and Islamic Sciences

This chapter provides a quick overview of Islamic sciences and their foundations. It is a quick review of Level 8.

Islam and Islamic Sciences

The Source of Islam

- Prophet Muhammad is the **ONLY** source of Islam for us, and he gave us this religion in two forms, which together form the corpus of religious knowledge.

Quran (Text)

- The last book of Islam
- Original text and language preserved
- Verbatim words of God
- Source of beliefs, moral guidelines, and some laws

Sunnah (Actions)

- Origin from Prophet Ibrahim
- Prophet Muhammad revived it, and now it is considered the Sunnah of Prophet Muhammad
- Source of most of the laws
- Traditions and practices are transmitted perpetually

> In terms of authenticity, there is no difference between the Quran and the Sunnah

The Content of Islam

Al-Hikmah

- The metaphysical and ethical basis of the worship prescribed by religion – matters of faith and morality.
- Remains the same for all prophets and their nations.
- **Example:** Be charitable.

Al-Kitab

- Contains the laws (Shariah) suitable for the time, along with rituals and limits.
- Changes due to evolution in human civilizations and societies.
- Current laws are based on the laws given to Prophet Ibrahim and have been shaped into the Prophet Muhammad's Sunnah since then.
- **Example:** Pay Zakah.

> "Islam" is also sometimes used to refer to the outer aspect of religion.

The Objective of Islam - Purification

- The entire content of religion and purification is always directly related.
- Every instruction given in the Quran and Sunnah is for one purpose: Tazkiyah (purification of oneself).
- It demands that our beliefs and deeds be developed in the right direction, which helps us attain purification.
- Our objective should be entering paradise, and according to the Quran, paradise is prepared for 'purified souls'.

Beliefs and Worship Rituals	←→	Purification of **Soul**
Dietary Laws	←→	Purification of **Food**
Laws for cleanliness	←→	Purification of **Body**
Guidance on Morality	←→	Purification of **Morals**

> There is no instruction, teaching, or law within Islam that is not targeted to achieve the objective of purification. If an instruction does not meet this criterion, it cannot be part of Islam.

Beliefs in Islam

Belief in God
- There is one True God, Allah, who is the Creator and Sustainer of everything.

Belief in Angels
- A creation of God who brings down and implements the directives and Will of God.

Belief in Prophets and Messengers
- God, through His all-encompassing knowledge and wisdom, selects human beings to guide mankind.

Belief in Divine Books
- Prophets are given books so that people/groups can resolve their differences through them and judge right from wrong.

Belief in the Day of Judgment and the Hereafter
- One day, we will be held accountable for our beliefs and actions in this world and will be rewarded accordingly.

Summary of Moral Teachings

10 Commandments
of Islam

Do not associate partners with God.

- Worship God alone.
- Be good with parents and relatives.
- Moderation in spending.
- Chastity and modesty.
- Sanctity of human life.

- Do not devour an orphan's wealth.
- Keep your promises.
- Be honest in your business.
- Do not follow speculations about others.
- Avoid pride and vanity.

Do not associate partners with God.

What is Shariah For?

Shariah, or Shariah Law, is the Islamic legal system derived from the two main religious sources of Islam: the Quran and the Sunnah.

- God gives Shariah to regulate the relationship, or covenant, between God and the believer, with the objective of purifying this relationship.
- Shariah guides a believer in various capacities and roles they hold (husband/wife, merchant, factory owner, leader of a nation, Prime Minister or President, etc.).
- The laws of Shariah apply only to Muslims in society.
- Even the criminal laws are given as a chastisement for breaking the covenant.
- For example, the law of inheritance is given so that believers do not commit injustice to their relatives. God gave them guidance on how to distribute the inheritance. It is not befitting for a believer, then, not to distribute their inheritance according to the law given by God, if they firmly believe that their God is All-Wise and must have given them the best guidance for distributing inheritance.

The Scope and Limits of Shariah

- It is a common misunderstanding that Islam provides a complete system in every domain of life (like financial, political, social, judicial, etc.)
- Contrary to that, only the fundamental guiding principles related to the laws in Shariah are given without any details – For example, it is not correct to say that Islam provides a "political system".
- The details of implementation are left to the human faculty of jurisprudence, so that different societies can apply the guiding principles of Shariah to different life situations, according to time and place.
- For example, Islam commands Muslims living in a society to form a state or government through mutual consultation. This principle can be applied in tribal cultures as well as in modern democracies, with differences in implementation details.
- Also, Shariah only covers a few critical circles of life where human beings, if left alone, can err and take extreme positions if not guided by God, as can be seen in some societies.

Fiqh and Ijtihad

Fiqh

- Application of Shariah to real-life situations where details in Shariah are missing.
- A human understanding of the Shariah is guided by the principles already given.
- There is some Fiqh in the Quran, and Prophet Muhammad provided such guidance during his lifetime.
- It is narrow in scope and applies to specific issues that depend on time, place, and circumstances.
- It can be changed when new information is available.
- Muslim jurists issue rulings on a given situation/matter, known as a fatwa.

Ijtihad

- An extension of Fiqh that applies to human efforts to understand and decide on matters not specified in the Quran and Sunnah.
- Matters explicitly stated in the Quran and Sunnah do not come under Ijtihad. If a matter is mentioned in the Quran and Sunnah, then deliberation on them is the right approach, not ijtihad.
- It is deduced from the relevant guiding principles already given in Shariah.
- This is usually done in matters that are new and for which there is no precedent. For example, organ donation.

Shariah	Fiqh	Ijtihad
God asks us to pray, and the basic method of praying is given through Sunnah.	Some details of praying that were left out (not mandatory). For example, should we raise our hands before going to the bowing position?	How to pray while flying in a plane and time zone keeps changing?
Asking for interest is prohibited on loans.	Can someone factor in the currency devaluation when asking for the loaned money back?	Is there an interest involved when someone buys a house on mortgage or how to purchase a house?
Generally, a dead Muslim should be bathed, clothed and, buried.	Are there differences between bathing men and women?	Organ donation.
Start and end your Ramadan when the new moon is sighted (whether on the 29th or 30th day).	How many people should witness the new moon before the start and the end of Ramadan can be announced?	Can a lunar calendar that is created with the help of accurate scientific data be used to start and end Ramadan?
Fasting is prescribed in Ramadan from dawn to dusk everyday.	What is the exact time when one should start and stop fasting?	How should people fast in Norway, where the sun does not set or rise for months?

Q & A and Discussion

Chapter 3

Relationship with Non-Muslims

This chapter discusses one of the most misunderstood topics among all the contemporary topics, and that is the nature of our relationship with non-Muslims.

Relationship with non-Muslims

Some Misconceptions

Before we get into the actual topic of the nature of our relationship with non-Muslims, let's first look into some misconceptions that will help us understand the topic well. For each misconception, a verse from the Quran or a Hadith is presented as evidence.

1. All non-Muslims are "Kafirs", worthy of condemnation and punishment.
2. It is not allowed to be friends with non-Muslims.

لَا يَتَّخِذِ الْمُؤْمِنُونَ الْكٰفِرِيْنَ اَوْلِيَآءَ مِنْ دُوْنِ الْمُؤْمِنِيْنَ

Believers should not make friends with disbelievers, leaving the believers aside. (3:28)

يٰٓاَيُّهَا الَّذِيْنَ اٰمَنُوْا لَا تَتَّخِذُوا الْكٰفِرِيْنَ اَوْلِيَآءَ مِنْ دُوْنِ الْمُؤْمِنِيْنَ اَتُرِيْدُوْنَ اَنْ تَجْعَلُوْا لِلّٰهِ عَلَيْكُمْ سُلْطٰنًا مُّبِيْنًا

Believers! Do not make friends with the disbelievers, leaving the believers aside. Do you wish to offer God an open argument against yourselves? (4:144)

يٰٓاَيُّهَا الَّذِيْنَ اٰمَنُوْا لَا تَتَّخِذُوا الْيَهُوْدَ وَ النَّصٰرٰى اَوْلِيَآءَ ۘ بَعْضُهُمْ اَوْلِيَآءُ بَعْضٍ ؕ وَ مَنْ يَّتَوَلَّهُمْ مِّنْكُمْ فَاِنَّهٗ مِنْهُمْ

Believers! Do not take these Jews and the Christians as your friends. They are but friends to each other. And he, amongst you, who turns to them [for friendship] is of them. (5:51)

3. Non-Muslims are permanently doomed to Hell in the Hereafter.
4. You cannot greet non-Muslims with Islamic greetings
5. It is not allowed to ask for forgiveness for non-Muslims from God.
6. A non-Muslim family member cannot inherit the wealth of a deceased Muslim.
7. If any one of the spouses becomes a Muslim or a non-Muslim, their marriage bond ends.

اِنَّ الَّذِيْنَ كَفَرُوْا مِنْ اَهْلِ الْكِتٰبِ وَ الْمُشْرِكِيْنَ فِيْ نَارِ جَهَنَّمَ خٰلِدِيْنَ فِيْهَا ؕ اُولٰٓئِكَ هُمْ شَرُّ الْبَرِيَّةِ

These Disbelievers among the People of the Book and the Idolaters shall burn forever in the fire of Hell. They are the vilest of all creatures. (98:6)

مَا كَانَ لِلنَّبِيِّ وَ الَّذِيْنَ اٰمَنُوْا اَنْ يَّسْتَغْفِرُوْا لِلْمُشْرِكِيْنَ وَ لَوْ كَانُوْا اُولِيْ قُرْبٰى مِنْ بَعْدِ مَا تَبَيَّنَ لَهُمْ اَنَّهُمْ اَصْحٰبُ الْجَحِيْمِ

It is not proper for the Prophet and those who believe in asking Allah's Forgiveness for these Idolaters, even though they are of kin, after it has become clear to them that they are the dwellers of the Fire. (9:113)

Abu Hurairah reported from the Prophet: "Don't initiate salutations to the Jews or the Christians." (Sahih Muslim #2167)

Usama ibn Zayd reported that the Prophet said: "A Muslim cannot be an heir to a Disbeliever, nor can a Disbeliever be a Muslim's heir. (Sahih Bukhari # 6383)

8. Testimony of non-Muslims cannot be accepted.
9. You cannot imitate non-Muslims in any aspect of life.
10. Non-Muslims should be treated as second-rate citizens (Dhimmi) in a Muslim society.

Ibn 'Umar said that the Prophet said: "I have been sent with the sword until God alone is worshipped, and my livelihood has been placed under the shade of my spear, and there is humiliation and subjugation for those who disobey me, and he who imitates a nation will be regarded from among them. (Musnad Ahmad # 5114)

Ibn 'Umar said that the Prophet said: "He who imitates a nation is from among them." (Sunan Abu Dawood #4031)

The Practice of God

- Many of these misconceptions arose from a lack of understanding of the Law of *Itmam Al-Hujjah* as described in the Quran.
- Among many practices described in the Quran, God, through natural disasters or the companions of Messengers, punishes and humiliates in this very world their foremost and direct addressees who deliberately deny the truth communicated to them by their respective messengers, and rewards in this very world those among them who adhere to the truth.
- In the second case, Messenger and his companions act as nothing but divine weapons, used to punish the disbelievers.
- It is God's retribution carried out by God Himself and must not be undertaken by human beings on their own.
- The purpose of this punishment is to remind mankind of the most important reality: the reward and punishment in the Hereafter will be based on a person's innate knowledge of good and evil, and on the divine message they received about God and their actions and deeds.

- This reality is substantiated visually by the Almighty through the agency of His Messengers in the form of the 'Day of Judgment on a smaller scale, for people to pay heed to those who come after them.
- This court of justice will be set up for every person on the Day of Judgment.
- The details of this practice are presented in the Quran in many places.
- The summary of this law is shown below:

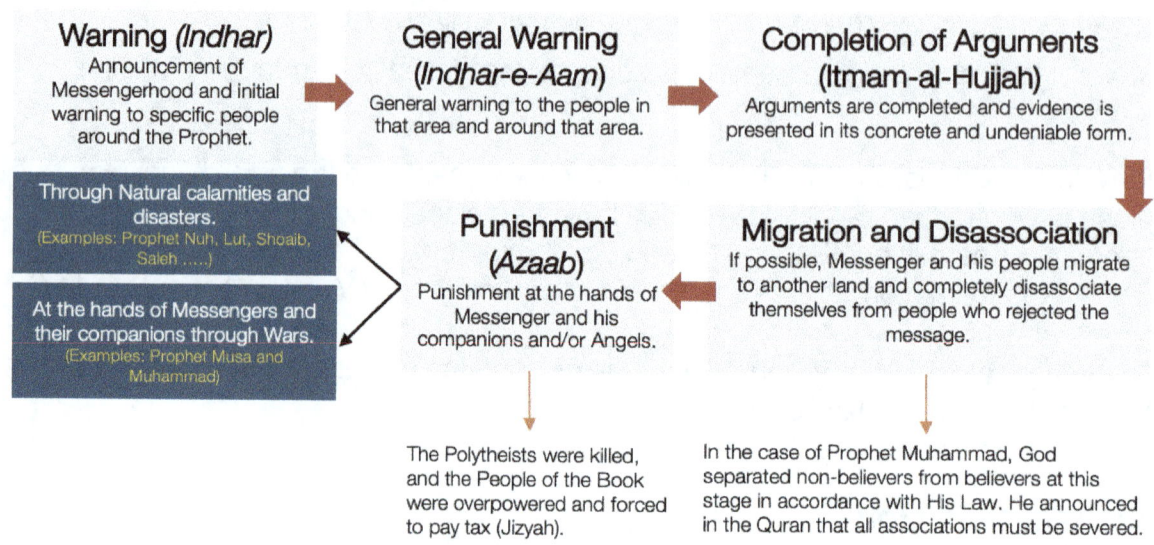

The law described in the Quran

اِنَّا اَوْحَيْنَا اِلَيْكَ كَمَا اَوْحَيْنَا اِلٰى نُوْحٍ وَّ النَّبِيّٖنَ مِنْ بَعْدِهٖ ۚ وَ اَوْحَيْنَا اِلٰى اِبْرٰهِيْمَ وَ اِسْمٰعِيْلَ وَ اِسْحٰقَ وَ يَعْقُوْبَ وَ الْاَسْبَاطِ وَ عِيْسٰى وَ اَيُّوْبَ وَ يُوْنُسَ وَ هٰرُوْنَ وَ سُلَيْمٰنَ ۚ وَ اٰتَيْنَا دَاوٗدَ زَبُوْرًا ۚ وَ رُسُلًا قَدْ قَصَصْنٰهُمْ عَلَيْكَ مِنْ قَبْلُ وَ رُسُلًا لَّمْ نَقْصُصْهُمْ عَلَيْكَ ۚ وَ كَلَّمَ اللّٰهُ مُوْسٰى تَكْلِيْمًا رُسُلًا مُّبَشِّرِيْنَ وَ مُنْذِرِيْنَ لِئَلَّا يَكُوْنَ لِلنَّاسِ عَلَى اللّٰهِ حُجَّةٌ بَعْدَ الرُّسُلِ ۚ وَ كَانَ اللّٰهُ عَزِيْزًا حَكِيْمًا

Surely, We have revealed to you as We revealed to Nuh, and the Prophets after him, and We revealed to Ibrahim and Ismail and Ishaq and Yaqoob and the tribes, and Isa and Ayyub and Younus and Haroun and Suleiman, and We gave to Dawood, Zaboor. And We have sent our revelations to those Messengers we have mentioned to you before, and also to the Messengers We have not mentioned to you, and Allah spoke to Musa the way it should be. (We have sent these) Messengers are the givers of good news and as warners, **so that people do not have an excuse in front of Allah** after the (coming of) Messengers; and Allah is Mighty, Wise. (Surah Nisa: 165-166)

- The Disbelievers of the Messengers are always punished in this world.

اَكُفَّارُكُمْ خَيْرٌ مِّنْ اُولٰئِكُمْ اَمْ لَكُمْ بَرَآءَةٌ فِى الزُّبُرِ اَمْ يَقُوْلُوْنَ نَحْنُ جَمِيْعٌ مُّنْتَصِرٌ سَيُهْزَمُ الْجَمْعُ وَ يُوَلُّوْنَ الدُّبُرَ

(O People of Quraysh), Are these disbelievers (among you) better than those (other nations we have just talked about), or do you have pardon written (for you) somewhere in the Scriptures? Do they think they are a group that will win against Us? (Listen), **This group will soon be defeated**, and they will show their backs.
(Surah Qamar:43)

قَاتِلُوْهُمْ يُعَذِّبْهُمُ اللهُ بِاَيْدِيْكُمْ وَ يُخْزِهِمْ وَ يَنْصُرْكُمْ عَلَيْهِمْ وَ يَشْفِ صُدُوْرَ قَوْمٍ مُّؤْمِنِيْنَ

Fight with them (Idolators), **Allah will punish them by your hands** and bring them to disgrace, and assist you against them and heal the hearts of believing people. (Surah Tawbah: 14)

قَاتِلُوا الَّذِيْنَ لَا يُؤْمِنُوْنَ بِاللهِ وَ لَا بِالْيَوْمِ الْاٰخِرِ وَ لَا يُحَرِّمُوْنَ مَا حَرَّمَ اللهُ وَ رَسُوْلُهُ وَ لَا يَدِيْنُوْنَ دِيْنَ الْحَقِّ مِنَ الَّذِيْنَ اُوْتُوا الْكِتٰبَ حَتّٰى يُعْطُوا الْجِزْيَةَ عَنْ يَّدٍ وَّ هُمْ صٰغِرُوْنَ

(Besides these Idolators) Fight with those (among People of the Book) who do not believe in Allah, nor the Day of Judgment, nor do they prohibit what Allah and His Messenger have prohibited, nor follow the religion of Truth, out of those who have been given the Book, until **they pay the tax in with their own hands while they are in a state of subjugation**. (Surah Tawbah: 29)

The Correct Perspective

Today's Non-Muslims are not idolaters and Kafirs addressed in the Quran.

- All such verses and Ahadith declaring some people Kafir, must be read in the context of the "Law of *Itmam al Hujjah*".
- These verses were revealed in the phase of the Prophetic mission when Muslims were asked to separate themselves as a collective group from the disbelievers.
- The disbelievers were soon to receive a divine punishment at the hands of the Muslims, and this disassociation was a precursor to that punishment.
- The Quran used the words Al Kafirin, Al Mushrikin, Al Yahud, Al Nasara – Al refers to the direct addressees of the Quran.
- The disassociation included not befriending them, not initiating greetings of peace, not marrying them, not applying the laws of inheritance to them, not asking for their forgiveness, not accepting their testimony, and not associating with them.

- The Punishment included all *Mushrikin*, who were supposed to be killed, and all Jews and Christians were allowed to accept the sovereignty of the Muslims and pay tax as a sign of subjugation.
- Both were promised a permanent punishment in the Hereafter for rejecting the truth after it was communicated conclusively through the messenger.

Some Key Points

- **Kafir:** Someone who has been presented the religion of Islam with undeniable evidence and he accepts in his heart that this is the Truth, but then denies or rejects it arrogantly (and publicly).

قَالَ الْمَلَأُ الَّذِينَ اسْتَكْبَرُوا مِنْ قَوْمِهِ لِلَّذِينَ اسْتُضْعِفُوا لِمَنْ اٰمَنَ مِنْهُمْ اَتَعْلَمُوْنَ اَنَّ صٰلِحًا مُّرْسَلٌ مِّنْ رَّبِّهٖ ۚ قَالُوْۤا اِنَّا بِمَاۤ اُرْسِلَ بِهٖ مُؤْمِنُوْنَ قَالَ الَّذِيْنَ اسْتَكْبَرُوۤا اِنَّا بِالَّذِيْۤ اٰمَنْتُمْ بِهٖ كٰفِرُوْنَ

The chief of those who behaved proudly among his people said to those who were considered weak, to those who believed from among them: Do you know that Salih is sent by his Lord? They said: Surely, we are believers in what he has been sent with. Those who were arrogant said: **Surely, we are rejectors** of what you believe in. (7:76)

- After Prophet Muhammad, there is no one on earth now who can decide if a person has rejected the Truth of Islam after accepting its Truth in their hearts.
- The crime of rejecting the Truth of Islam or associating partners with God is related to God and not to society or an individual.
- The killing of the idolaters was a part of the divine punishment.
- The narrations attributed to Prophet Muhammad in this regard must be understood in light of the Quran, which explains the Law of *Itmam al-Hujjah* in detail.
- People who reject the faith or associate partners with God deliberately will meet their fate on the Day of Judgment. They will be judged on their efforts to seek the Truth, their understanding of the Message, and the factors taken into account in their rejection.
- There is nothing wrong with asking for guidance for non-Muslims when they are alive and praying for God's mercy on them when they die.
- After *Itmam ul Hujjah*, Muslims were directed to boycott their disbelieving relatives so they could not inherit from each other. While the Quran states that the law of inheritance (Quran 4:12) rests on "the benefit associated with kinship," it must be practiced today regardless of religion.

يَٰٓأَيُّهَا ٱلَّذِينَ ءَامَنُوٓا۟ إِذَا ضَرَبْتُمْ فِى سَبِيلِ ٱللَّهِ فَتَبَيَّنُوا۟ وَ لَا تَقُولُوا۟ لِمَنْ أَلْقَىٰٓ إِلَيْكُمُ ٱلسَّلَٰمَ لَسْتَ مُؤْمِنًا ۚ تَبْتَغُونَ عَرَضَ ٱلْحَيَوٰةِ ٱلدُّنْيَا ۚ فَعِندَ ٱللَّهِ مَغَانِمُ كَثِيرَةٌ ۚ كَذَٰلِكَ كُنتُم مِّن قَبْلُ فَمَنَّ ٱللَّهُ عَلَيْكُمْ فَتَبَيَّنُوٓا۟ ۚ إِنَّ ٱللَّهَ كَانَ بِمَا تَعْمَلُونَ خَبِيرًا

O you who believe! When you go to war in Allah's way, investigate, and do not say to anyone who offers you *Salam*: You are not a believer. Do you seek the benefits of this world's life? But with Allah there are abundant gains; you too were such before, then Allah conferred a favor upon you; but investigate; surely Allah is aware of what you do. (4:94)

- In the time of the Prophet (PBUH), non-Muslims were not trusted for a testimony, as there was a conflict going on between believers and non-believers, and non-believers had all the intentions to harm believers.
- Jews, Christians, hypocrites, and Idolaters were living with Muslims in the same locality with no distinction between them – God made certain aspects of Islam as the differentiating factor for being a Muslim or sometimes as a true believer.
  - For example, coming to the mosque to pray in congregation
  - Saying Islamic greetings "Assalam O Alaikum"
  - Establishing Prayers (Quran 9:11)
  - Paying of Zakat (Quran 9:11)
- Marrying idolaters was prohibited for Muslims. However, Muslim men were allowed to marry the women of the people of the Book, i.e., Jews and Christians. This exception was given at a time when Muslims were a dominating political force in Arabia.

وَلَا تَنكِحُوا۟ ٱلْمُشْرِكَٰتِ حَتَّىٰ يُؤْمِنَّ ۚ وَلَأَمَةٌ مُّؤْمِنَةٌ خَيْرٌ مِّن مُّشْرِكَةٍ وَلَوْ أَعْجَبَتْكُمْ ۗ وَلَا تُنكِحُوا۟ ٱلْمُشْرِكِينَ حَتَّىٰ يُؤْمِنُوا۟ ۚ وَلَعَبْدٌ مُّؤْمِنٌ خَيْرٌ مِّن مُّشْرِكٍ وَلَوْ أَعْجَبَكُمْ ۗ أُو۟لَٰٓئِكَ يَدْعُونَ إِلَى ٱلنَّارِ ۖ وَٱللَّهُ يَدْعُوٓا۟ إِلَى ٱلْجَنَّةِ وَٱلْمَغْفِرَةِ بِإِذْنِهِۦ ۖ وَيُبَيِّنُ ءَايَٰتِهِۦ لِلنَّاسِ لَعَلَّهُمْ يَتَذَكَّرُونَ

And [even for the orphans' welfare] do not marry Idolatrous women unless they believe. And [remember that] a believing slave girl is better than an Idolatrous woman, although you may like her. And do not also marry your women to the Idolaters unless they believe. And [remember that] a believing slave is better than an Idolater, although you may like him. They call you to Hell, and God, by His grace, invites you to Paradise and forgiveness and explains His revelations to people so they may take heed. (2:221)

الْيَوْمَ أُحِلَّ لَكُمُ الطَّيِّبَاتُ ۖ وَطَعَامُ الَّذِينَ أُوتُوا الْكِتَابَ حِلٌّ لَّكُمْ وَطَعَامُكُمْ حِلٌّ لَّهُمْ ۖ وَالْمُحْصَنَاتُ مِنَ الْمُؤْمِنَاتِ وَالْمُحْصَنَاتُ مِنَ الَّذِينَ أُوتُوا الْكِتَابَ مِن قَبْلِكُمْ إِذَا آتَيْتُمُوهُنَّ أُجُورَهُنَّ مُحْصِنِينَ غَيْرَ مُسَافِحِينَ وَلَا مُتَّخِذِي أَخْدَانٍ ۗ وَمَن يَكْفُرْ بِالْإِيمَانِ فَقَدْ حَبِطَ عَمَلُهُ وَهُوَ فِي الْآخِرَةِ مِنَ الْخَاسِرِينَ

All pure things have now been made lawful to you. The food of the People of the Book is lawful to you and yours to them. Similarly, lawful to you are the chaste women of the Muslims and those who were given the Book before you when you give them their dowers with the condition that you too desire chastity, not lewdness nor becoming secret paramours. [Bear in mind that] those who reject faith, all their hard work ended up in vain, and in the Hereafter, they will be among the losers. (5:5)

- Today, however, if either spouse changes his or her faith, the marriage bond does not automatically break because there is no ruling to that effect. It is the spouses' choice to decide whether to continue living together or separate. For example, a Muslim spouse may decide to separate because the other spouse is doing open Shirk with God (for example, a follower of Hinduism).

- Regarding the imitation of non-Muslims, there is a general principle to consider. Imitation in matters of faith, religious practices, and associating with them against the interest of Muslims of Islam is forbidden, but following cultural practices, etc., there are no restrictions, except that there is a chance that Muslims would get involved in some polytheistic or unethically wrong practices.

Dealing with Non-Muslims

- Regardless of religion, our first unbreakable bond that we have with other human beings is the human bond (they are also the children of Adam). The rights and obligations that emanate from this relationship are binding upon us. In that relationship they are our brothers and sisters in humanity.

- For example, a non-Muslim neighbor is a neighbor first and then a non-Muslim. All the rights that a neighbor has upon us must be fulfilled.

- On top of that we have another responsibility which is to convey the message and the news of that big event that Prophets and Messengers have warned us against, i.e. the event of the Day of Judgment and the life in the Hereafter.

- If we truly believe in this, then this is our responsibility to convey this message to them also. This makes them the invitee of our message.

- However, we must use wisdom and the right judgment when and how to invite them.

Q & A and Discussion

Chapter 4

Jihad and Militancy

This chapter discusses one of the most misused concepts in Islam: Jihad. It has been misused by Muslims more than anyone else without properly understanding it from the Quran.

Jihad in Islam

Introduction

- Jihad is the most misunderstood directive of Islam, which has been misused by certain groups of Muslims in different parts of the world.
- These groups are often ideologically motivated, have political, economic, or societal grievances, and tend to use religion to recruit people and justify their atrocities.
- The tactics used by such groups in the name of Jihad often produce indiscriminate violence that targets innocent people.
- These acts have created the greatest misunderstanding about Islam, and that is, 'it is an inherently violent religion that condones violence and acts of terrorism.
- Islam categorically prohibits such actions in all their shapes and forms and reveals extraordinary respect for human life in the Quran (Surah Maida:32).
- The objective of warfare in Islam, with all its limits and bounds, is to end religious persecution and oppression at the collective level.
- This concept has been misused so much so that now most people equate terrorism and Jihad despite the fact that it is one of the most virtuous acts in Islam, as it requires both financial and personal sacrifices for the sake of Allah.

Jihad ≠ Terrorism

The main misconceptions

1. It is the duty of Muslim Authorities to conduct Jihad against the polytheists as well as the Jewish and Christian nations. Polytheists must be killed, and Jews/Christians must be subdued.
2. The non-Muslim citizens of an Islamic state will be considered second-rate citizens called Dhimmis (those who live under an Islamic state and pay a specific tax, Jizyah).
3. Muslim groups and organizations can conduct Jihad against such people without the state authority, in case the state is not willing to do so.
4. The following verses are usually presented as evidence:

فَإِذَا انْسَلَخَ الْأَشْهُرُ الْحُرُمُ فَاقْتُلُوا الْمُشْرِكِينَ حَيْثُ وَجَدْتُمُوهُمْ وَ خُذُوهُمْ وَ احْصُرُوهُمْ وَ اقْعُدُوا لَهُمْ كُلَّ مَرْصَدٍ ۚ

فَإِنْ تَابُوا وَ أَقَامُوا الصَّلوةَ وَ أَتَوُا الزَّكوةَ فَخَلُّوا سَبِيلَهُمْ ۚ إِنَّ اللهَ غَفُورٌ رَّحِيمٌ

So, when the sacred months have passed, then slay the idolaters wherever you find them, and take them captives and besiege them and lie in wait for them in every ambush, then if they repent and keep up Prayers and pay Zakah, leave their way; surely Allah forgives, Merciful. (9:5)

قَاتِلُوا الَّذِينَ لَا يُؤْمِنُونَ بِاللهِ وَ لَا بِالْيَوْمِ الْآخِرِ وَ لَا يُحَرِّمُونَ مَا حَرَّمَ اللهُ وَ رَسُولُ وَ لَا يَدِينُونَ دِينَ الْحَقِّ مِنَ الَّذِينَ أُوتُوا الْكِتْبَ حَتَّى يُعْطُوا الْجِزْيَةَ عَنْ يَّدٍ وَّ بُمْ صُغِرُونَ

Fight with those (among People of the Book) who do not believe in Allah, nor the Day of Judgment, nor do they prohibit what Allah and His Messenger have prohibited, nor follow the religion of Truth, out of those who have been given the Book, until they pay the tax in with their own hands while they are in a state of subjugation (9:29)

فَقَاتِلُوا أَئِمَّةَ الْكُفْرِ ۖ إِنَّهُمْ لَا آيَمَانَ لَهُمْ لَعَلَّهُمْ يَنْتَهُونَ

Then fight with these leaders of disbelief. The oath or words have no significance (they will ultimately break it), so fight until they cease (to disbelieve) (9:12)

Fatwa Issued by Jihadi Groups

- In February 1998, Osama bin Laden and leaders from other militant groups (including Ayman al-Zawahiri) issued a concise and aggressive fatwa under the banner of the "World Islamic Front for Jihad Against Jews and Crusaders".
- Expanded Mandate: This fatwa declared that killing Westerners and their allies—both civilians and military—was an "individual duty" for every Muslim who was able to do so in any country where it was possible.
- Three Main Pillars: The statement cited three specific reasons for this order:
  - The ongoing "occupation" of the Arabian Peninsula by Western forces.
  - The "great devastation" inflicted on the Iraqi people by Western sanctions.
  - Western support for the "Zionist-Crusader" alliance and the occupation of Jerusalem.
- Defensive Jihad: Bin Laden framed these attacks as a "defensive struggle" to protect the Muslim community (Ummah) from perceived Western aggression.
- They quoted the very same verses of the Quran in their Fatwa.

Source: EBSCO

Jihad against Non-Muslims

- All the verses presented in support of the argument specifically pertain to the Idolaters, the Jews, and the Christians of the Prophet Muhammad's time, as per the Law of Itmam al Hujjah (for more details, please see slides for "Dealing with Non-Muslims").
- All the directives related to the fighting and killing of the leaders of the Quraysh must be understood in the light of the context of this Divine Law, also known as "*Sunnatullah*."
- The wars fought by the Prophet and his companions (after his death) were undertaken solely to complete God's divine scheme, resulting in the punishment of the Prophet's direct addressees.
- These wars were not fought for:
  - Spreading the message of Islam.
  - The expansion of the geographical boundaries.
- These directives cannot be extended to people after them.
- In today's world of nation-states, the relationship between a Muslim state and a non-Muslim state is defined by international agreements signed by all countries on the platform of the United Nations, and Muslim nations must abide by those agreements.

When is War allowed in Islam?

- If we carefully read the Quran, it will be quite clear to us that Allah permitted fighting because of only reasons:
- **Against Injustice and Oppression** – This is a general category in which Muslims are asked to use force against people who are using violence to curb the basic rights of human beings. This is an eternal directive in Shariah, valid for all times and places.

And had it not been that Allah dislodge one nation through another, the monasteries and churches, the synagogues and the mosques, in which His praise is abundantly celebrated, would be utterly destroyed. (22:40)

- **Against the Rejecters of the Truth** – This category falls outside Shariah and pertains to the divine law of *Itmam al-Hujjah*, in which God punishes nations for rejecting the truth through the hands of Messengers and their companions once evidence is presented in clear terms. This is not relevant after Prophet Muhammad.

وَ لِكُلِّ أُمَّةٍ رَّسُولٌ ۖ فَإِذَا جَاءَ رَسُولُهُمْ قُضِىَ بَيْنَهُم بِالْقِسْطِ وَ هُمْ لَا يُظْلَمُونَ

And for each community, there is a Messenger. Then, when their Messenger comes, their fate is decided with justice, and they are not wronged. (10:47)

The Status of Non-Muslims in a Muslim-Majority Land

- Since Muslims did not 'conquer' any of the lands where they have a majority now, the non-Muslims residing in these lands will be considered citizens of that land/country with equal political rights.
- The Non-Muslims of a Muslim-majority land cannot be considered second-rate citizens anymore and are required to pay Jizyah for the protection.
- For religious matters and laws, the Muslim-majority state can maintain a contract with the non-Muslim minority, keeping in view the general welfare of the state and the people.
- Any such contract agreed between them must comply with international agreements and pacts.
- At the individual level, all non-Muslims are now "callees," and we are the "callers" of Islam (towards Allah SWT).

War without Authority

أُذِنَ لِلَّذِينَ يُقَاتَلُونَ بِأَنَّهُمْ ظُلِمُوا ۚ وَ إِنَّ اللهَ عَلَى نَصْرِهِمْ لَقَدِيرٌ الَّذِينَ أُخْرِجُوا مِن دِيَارِهِم بِغَيْرِ حَقٍّ إِلَّا أَن يَقُولُوا رَبُّنَا اللهُ

Permission to take up arms is hereby granted to those who are attacked because they have been oppressed, and God indeed has the power to help them – those who have been unjustly driven from their homes, only because they said: "Our Lord is Allah." **(22:39-40)**

- As can be seen from the above verses, the right to use force is given to the Muslims in their collective capacity.
- Among many directives given to a state, waging war against a group of people (including countries) is one of those directives, and does not address Muslims in their individual capacity.
- These verses were revealed to the Muslims after they had established political authority in Medina.
- The Prophet has also described it in many Ahadith.

إِنَّمَا الْإِمَامُ جُنَّةٌ يُقَاتَلُ مِنْ وَرَائِهِ وَيُتَّقَى بِهِ

A Muslim ruler is the shield [of his people]. An armed struggle can only be carried out under him, and people should seek his shelter [in war] (Sahih Bukhari #2797)

عَنْ مَكْحُولٍ عَنْ أَبِي هُرَيْرَةَ قَالَ قَالَ رَسُولُ اللَّهِ صَلَّى اللَّهُ عَلَيْهِ وَسَلَّمَ الْجِهَادُ وَاجِبٌ عَلَيْكُمْ مَعَ كُلِّ أَمِيرٍ بَرًّا كَانَ أَوْ فَاجِرًا

Makhul narrates from Abu Hurairah, who narrates from the Prophet: Jihad is obligatory on you only in the presence of a Muslim ruler, whether he is pious or impious. (Abu Dawood, Sunan, vol. 3, 18, (no. 2533)

- Waging Jihad without a political authority is a new phenomenon; otherwise, there is a consensus among all scholars of Islam that only a Muslim state has the authority to wage Jihad.

من الفروض الكفائية ما يشترط فيه الحاكم مثل: الجهاد وإقامة الحدود

Among collective obligations, there is a category for which the existence of a ruler is necessary, e.g., Jihad and administering punishments (Sayyid Sabiq in Fiqh us-Sunnah vol 3, page 30)

والسادس : جهاد من عاند الإسلام

And his sixth obligation is to conduct Jihad against those who show hostility against Islam (Al Mawardi, A Shafiite Scholar, wrote in Al Ahkam Al Sultaniyyah, page 52)

وأمر الجهاد موكول إلى الإمام واجتهاده ويلزم الرعية طاعته فيما يراه
من ذلك

And the matter of jihad rests with the ruler [of a state] and his Ijtihad. The opinion he forms in this regard must be obeyed by the citizens of his country (Ibn Qudamah, A Hanbali Scholar, wrote in Al Mughni, vol 8, page 352)

Conditions for Jihad

- Any state/government or group that wants to wage Jihad must fulfill the following conditions:

Nature of obligation

- Must be executed under an independent Islamic state with political authority in the land.
- The military might of the Muslims must be up to a certain level, with the confidence that they will win. If this condition is missing, then the war is allowed but not mandated by Allah.
- God has promised help in a just war according to the moral strength of the Muslims (Quran 8:65, 8:66).

The Driving Force

- Must be undertaken <u>ONLY</u> for causes set forth by God, e.g., against persecution.
- God promises a great reward for such a war.
- It cannot be waged for gratifying one's whims, obtaining wealth, conquering lands, or for fame.
- It cannot be waged today, even to spread Islam or make it dominant over other religions.

Ethical limits

- Basic ethics and morality must prevail even during a chaotic situation like war.
- Treaties and pacts must not be broken unless an open breach is observed.
- The damage/harm must be inflicted in proportion to the violation of rights, and all kinds of excesses must be avoided.
- Extra care must be taken to avoid civilian casualties.
- People who do not want to fight or remain neutral must be left alone.

Ultimate goal

- To uproot persecution (limited to Jihad not associated with Messengers).
- All kinds of persecutions must be targeted, but especially religious persecution.
- All options for negotiations and talks must be considered before deciding on the war.

Any Jihad undertaken by the religious groups in a country will only result in creating corruption and disorder in the land, as there will be no political authority to stop the followers from committing war crimes and excesses. This has been witnessed multiple times in recent history. The same people who waged war against the "disbelievers" later fought with each other for supremacy on the land.

The Jihad of the Companions of Prophet Muhammad

Some people raise this concern: "*Itmam-al-Hujjah* can be accepted for individuals who were the direct addressees of the Prophet, as he totally convinced them regarding the message of Islam, and they deliberately denied the truth. But what about the nations (i.e., Persians and Romans) that were just sent letters? Can *Itmam al hujjah* be done just by sending letters, and why did the companions of the Prophet continue to wage Jihad against these nations?"

- The Messengers are sent to the center of a civilization known to the people and regions around it. The Quran called it "*Ummul Quraa*" (Mother/center of the cities).
- Regarding the Itmam-al-Hujjah with neighboring countries during the time of the Prophet, it was not merely accomplished by writing letters. Letters were just one of the methods used to conduct *Itmam-al-Hujjah*.
- The real event for them was the occurrence of the *Shahadah* of Prophet Muhammad in Arabia. They were witnessing it and were fully aware of it. Various dialogues, now part of history, between Muslims and these rulers suggest the same.
- They were also aware of the humiliating defeat of Quraysh at the hands of a handful of Muslims. This was enough to conclusively convey the truth to the rulers of neighboring countries to whom the Prophet wrote these letters.
- Any evasion on their part was tantamount to a deliberate denial of the truth. As a result, they had to face the wrath of God in the form of attacks launched by the Companions after the Prophet's departure.
- The common masses of these countries were also observers of the divine judgment which took place in Arabia, and hence to them also the truth was conclusively conveyed.
- Any individual inquiry from them about the truth would, of course, have been treated in the same manner as it was in the case of Idolaters of Arabia. Many delegations from these Kingdoms came and met Prophet Muhammad before his death.
- Since Allah wanted to give victory and dominance to Islam in that region as His sign for the last Messenger on earth, He ordered the companions to remove any threat from the lands that surrounded the land of Arabia.

Q & A and Discussion

Chapter 5

Democracy or Caliphate

This chapter discusses the concept of Caliphate, given the history of Muslim rulership, and where modern democracy fits into the picture.

Democracy or Caliphate

Introduction

- For some fourteen centuries, Islam and the Muslim world had been synonymous with the caliphate, and after the downfall of the Ottoman Empire, several movements and groups struggled (one way or the other) to restore that 'glory'.
- Historically, the Islamic Caliphate was considered a symbol of Islam's supremacy.
- There is a debate among the scholars of Islam about whether the current state of the Muslims and the Islamic world has something to do with the loss of the Caliphate and whether the only way for Muslims to improve the situation is to strive for its return, or in other words, strive for the supremacy of Islam.
- Some scholarly circles believe that Islam has asked every Muslim to strive to establish an Islamic state in the country where they are living, in case the affairs are not managed according to Islam (the ideal is to have one Islamic state in the world).
- There is also a dichotomy among scholars about whether Islam and democracy are compatible, and the main reason for this debate is the association of liberalism and secularism with democratic values and culture.

Does Islam mandate the Caliphate (Khilafah)?

- It is evident from the Quran and Ahadith that the words "Khilafah" and "Khalifah" are not religious terms at all, and in both contexts they are used in their general sense with different shades of meaning–as subordinate, successor, and/or ruler.
- As can be seen in a verse of the Quran, God used this word for Prophet Daud when he made him king of Bani Israel.
- The same word was used to refer to a successor when Abu Bakr took the reins of the Muslims.
- It is interesting to note that after the first 30 years of Islam, when Muslims rulership moved towards Kingdoms and Sultanates, the ruler was still called the Khalifah.

We said, "O David, indeed, We have made you a ruler on this earth, so judge between the people in truth and do not follow (your) desire (Surah Saad: 26)

When Abu Bakr became Khalifah, he was called "*Khalifatu Rasool Allah*" (the successor of the Messenger of Allah). When he died, and Omar became Khalifah, he was called "*Khalifatu Khalifati Rasool Allah*" (the successor of the successor of the Messenger of Allah). So, he chose "*Ameer ul Mumineen*" as the title for himself. (History of Islam)

- Regarding the form of Government, the Quran is quiet on the matter. However, it gave us the fundamental principle that should be kept in consideration when forming any government.
- The reason is that it is one of those matters that will change over time, and new forms of government will be adopted in response to the circumstances and developments the world has undergone.

وَ اَمْرُهُمْ شُوْرٰى بَيْنَهُمْ

"And their (Muslims) collective issues will be managed through mutual consultation." (Al-Shura:38)

- For this reason, Islam did not recommend any form of government and left it to collective wisdom, as long as the guiding principle is kept in mind, unless there is a valid reason to abandon it and take a less preferrable approach (other than mutual consultation)

Islam and Democracy

- As stated earlier, the guiding principle that the Quran has given about forming the government or selecting/removing a leader is "it should be done through mutual consultation" – in its rudimentary form, that is, democracy, which can be implemented in different ways in different societies.
- In the simplest terms, democracy is a method by which common people decide through a voting process when there are multiple options to choose from – a group of common people may choose someone as a representative to participate on their behalf in that decision-making.
- To practice this fundamental principle, the following aspects become necessary:
  1. People should be given absolute freedom to express their consent in all matters related to the decision.
  2. Consent obtained through force, intimidation, greed, gratification, deception, and fraud cannot be considered consent at all.
  3. This should go both ways: decisions should be made with mutual consultation, and if there is a need to undo them, that should also be done with mutual consultation.
  4. The decisions made through this process must enjoy the confidence of the majority.

5. The group in the minority must accept the decision with full hearts until the next opportunity to vote again – during this time, they must have complete freedom to criticize the decision and express their dissent.
6. There is no room for dictatorship.
7. There is no room for one section of society to rule the masses.

Ruler has the right to overrule the majority?

So, ignore their faults, ask for God's forgiveness, and consult them in the affairs [of state]. Then, when you have made a decision, put your trust in Allah. (Surah Aal-e-Imran:159)

- It is usually construed from this verse that the head of a Muslim state can overrule the majority through a veto.
- If we read the verse in its context, it becomes evident that it addresses a specific situation during the Battle of Uhud, involving a particular group: the hypocrites (who wanted to fight while remaining in Medina rather than going out to fight).
- The Prophet was asked to include them in the mutual consultation and not cut them off until God's decision about them is revealed in the Quran (for example, Surah Tahrim, Verse 9).
- However, the Prophet (in his capacity of being a prophet) was not bound to do what the majority says, and if he decides on something, he and Muslims should repose their trust in Allah and must carry on with their decision.
- Historically, it is known that the hypocrites who stayed with the Muslims in Uhud started spreading the propaganda that "the defeat was due to the wrong strategy adopted."
- Because the addressee of this verse is Prophet Muhammad (who is directly guided by God) and he was given instructions about a specific group of his time (hypocrites), the verse cannot be used as evidence for the veto power of a Muslim ruler.

Should Muslims strive for the supremacy of Islam?

It is He Who has sent His Rasul with guidance and the religion of Truth that he may proclaim it (dominate) over all religions, even though the Idolaters may detest [this]. (61:9)

- In light of the verse above, many groups of Muslims consider it a religious obligation to strive for the supremacy of Islam in the world, regardless of their status in the land (majority or minority), which should result in a single Islamic state – they term it "Islamic Revolution".
- An analysis of the context of this verse in light of the divine practice of "*Itmam-al-Hujjah*" shows that it relates to the mission given to Prophet Muhammad.
- The word "*Al Mushrikun*" refers to the idolaters of Arabia in the Prophet's time. A similar topic is repeated in other verses, which end up in a statement like "even though the disbelievers may detest." – In all these verses, Al (Alif Laam) is the Alif Laam of time and space.
- In light of the above explanation, "all the religions" can only mean all the religions of Arabia at that time.
- The verse has no bearing on Muslims after the time of Prophet Muhammad, and Muslims are not required by their religion to fulfill any such obligation.

The Example of Prophet Muhammad

وَعَدَ اللهُ الَّذِيْنَ اٰمَنُوْا مِنْكُمْ وَ عَمِلُوا الصّٰلِحٰتِ لَيَسْتَخْلِفَنَّهُمْ فِي الْاَرْضِ كَمَا اسْتَخْلَفَ الَّذِيْنَ مِنْ قَبْلِهِمْ ۫ وَ لَيُمَكِّنَنَّ لَهُمْ دِيْنَهُمُ الَّذِى ارْتَضٰى لَهُمْ

God has promised those among you who believed and did righteous deeds that He will surely grant them political authority in this land as He granted it to those before them; He will establish their religion – which He has chosen for them. (24:55)

اِنَّ الَّذِيْنَ يُحَآدُّوْنَ اللهَ وَ رَسُوْلَهٗ اُولٰٓئِكَ فِي الْاَذَلِّيْنَ ۛ كَتَبَ اللهُ لَاَغْلِبَنَّ اَنَا وَ رُسُلِيْ ۛ اِنَّ اللهَ قَوِيٌّ عَزِيْزٌ

Indeed, those who oppose Allah and His Messenger are bound to be humiliated. The Almighty has ordained: "My messengers and I shall always prevail." Indeed, Allah is Mighty and Powerful. (58:20-21)

- Some religious scholars cite the example of the Prophet and his companions establishing an "Islamic State" or authority in Arabia.
- It is evident from verses 24:55, 58:20-21, and similar verses in the Quran that the companions of the Prophet were promised sovereignty over the land of Arabia as a reward (God-gifted) for believing in him, whereas those who rejected him received punishment (Azab).
- The Prophet and his companions never undertook the task of establishing an Islamic state, nor did the Almighty direct him to do so – God bestowed authority upon them to make His religion supreme in the land, as mentioned in verse 61:9.

Q & A and Discussion

Chapter 6

Punishment for Apostasy

This chapter discusses the concept of Apostasy and its punishment, which is prevalent in most Muslim countries. We will try to understand its true placement in the history of Islam.

Punishment for Apostasy

Introduction

- One of the laws in Islamic countries (at least on paper) that generates a lot of criticism from modern societies is the death penalty for Apostasy (leaving the religion of Islam).
- According to the critics, Islam does not entertain any freedom of religion for human beings.
- On the other hand, they admit that millions of non-Muslims continued to live under Islamic rule without being forced to change their religion.
- This law must be understood in the light of the development of modern societies, where the role of religion has dramatically diminished in the law and governance.
- In modern democracies like the US, everyone has the right to practice their religion or no religion at all, and this is considered one of the fundamental rights of a human being.

What is Apostasy?

According to Wikipedia, apostasy in Muslim law, known as *Riddah* or *Irtidad*, is the conscious abandonment of Islam by a Muslim, either through explicit renunciation, converting to another religion, or denying fundamental tenets of faith. This leaves no room for a person to leave Islam once they have accepted it, whether they want to remain a Muslim or not.

General Understanding

- According to almost all Jurists of Islam, a Muslim who leaves the fold of Islam is punishable by death.

قال النبي صلى الله عليه وسلم مَنْ بَدَّلَ دِينَهُ فَاقْتُلُوهُ

The Prophet said: "Execute the people who change their faith." (Sahih Bukhari #2854)

- They consider this instruction applicable at all times to all Muslims.
- All the laws of Apostasy made in Islamic countries are based on this single hadith.
- Those Jurists who consider Islam as a political power in which human beings are the representatives of God (Vicegerent) on earth view apostasy as a crime of treason against the Islamic state, which is punishable by death.
- It is important to note that the Quran does not specifically mention this.

The right perspective

- Reminding his mission among the people of Quraysh, Prophet Muhammad has been reported to have said:

أُمِرْتُ أَنْ أُقَاتِلَ النَّاسَ حَتَّى يَشْهَدُوا أَنْ لاَ إِلَهَ إِلاَّ اللَّهُ وَأَنَّ مُحَمَّدًا رَسُولُ اللَّهِ وَيُقِيمُوا الصَّلاَةَ وَيُؤْتُوا الزَّكَاةَ فَإِذَا فَعَلُوا عَصَمُوا مِنِّي دِمَاءَهُمْ وَأَمْوَالَهُمْ إِلاَّ بِحَقِّهَا وَحِسَابُهُمْ عَلَى اللَّهِ

Abdullah ibn Umar reports from the Prophet: "I have been directed to fight against these people until they testify to the oneness of God and the prophethood of Muhammad, are diligent in the Prayer, and pay Zakah. If they accept these terms, their lives will be spared except if they commit some other violation that entails their execution by Islamic law, and [in the Hereafter] their account rests with God. (Sahih Muslim #22)

- In Sunan Al Kubra, Al Nisai recorded a similar hadith, which indicates that "these people" refers to "Al Mushrikeen". (Al Sunan Al Kubra #3428)
- The Ahadith are the historical record of Prophet Muhammad's statements, actions, and approvals, and are not an independent source of religious directives. All Ahadith must be understood in the light of the Quran.
- These two Ahadith must be understood in the context of the "Law of *Itmam Al Hujjah*" (for more details, please check the chapter on "Dealing with Non-Muslims").
- The hadith that is quoted is merely a statement associated with the Law of *Itmam al Hujjah* for the Arab Idolators of the Prophet's time.
- It is not even related to the People of the Book of that time.
- The hadith describes a situation in which an Idolator may have accepted Islam to save his life, as punishment was already prescribed for him, but then reverted to his original state of disbelief once the situation is more suitable for him.
- Since the punishment of death was prescribed by Allah for the disbelievers of Quraysh, they will get that punishment if they try to revert even immediately after the passing of the Prophet Muhammad.
- That's why Abu Bakr fought a war with the people who refused to deposit Zakah to the state, as it was one of the conditions to remain Muslim at that time.

The onslaught launched by the first caliph, Abu Bakr, against those who had refused to pay Zakah in his time should also be understood in this perspective and is a good implementation of this hadith. Since, according to Islam, a person who refuses to pay Zakah does not legally remain a Muslim, those who had evaded Zakah from among the Idolaters had reverted to their state of disbelief. About them, the directive was either to accept faith or face death. So, the caliph Abu Bakr was merely administering the punishment of death upon them as per the law of Itmam al Hujjah. (History of Islam)

Some Key Points

There is no compulsion in the matter of religion (from God). In reality, (it is not needed because after this Quran) the guidance has been clearly separated from the misguidance. (2:256)

- This life is a trial and a test for us in matters of our beliefs (knowledge) and our actions (good vs evil).

- Death ends this test, and it is only God's Jurisdiction to decide when a person's time for this test is over – for the Messenger's direct addressees, this is decided by God in accordance with His law.

- Any coercion in the matter of belief also fails the purpose of this test.

- It seems contradictory that Islam invites people to embrace it and then declares death punishment for someone who wants to revert to another faith.

- The Quran has given this freedom of conscience and choice of religious belief on many occasions. It does suggest the punishment in the Hereafter, but no worldly punishment is mentioned.

- No hadith or narration of Prophet Muhammad should be understood in isolation, but in the light of the Quran. In this case, if we consider that apostates should be punished by death, then it is in complete contradiction with many of the verses of the Quran where Allah told Prophet Muhammad not to act as a guardian over people, and Allah will guide them as per His law of guidance.

- Similarly, in many places in the Quran, Allah gave full freedom to accept or reject Allah's message until the punishment is decided. Punishment is the result, not coercion to accept the message.

إِنَّا هَدَيْنُهُ السَّبِيلَ إِمَّا شَاكِرًا وَّ إِمَّا كَفُوْرًا

We have shown him the paths (for good and evil); now it's his choice to be grateful (believe) or ungrateful (disbelieve). (76:2)

وَ نَفْسٍ وَّ مَا سَوّٰىهَا   فَاَلْهَمَهَا فُجُوْرَهَا وَ تَقْوٰىهَا   قَدْ اَفْلَحَ مَنْ زَكّٰىهَا   وَ قَدْ خَابَ مَنْ دَسّٰىهَا

And by the Soul and how We have fashioned it. Then, We revealed both evil and good in it. So, he is successful (on the Day of Judgment) who has purified it, and he is a failure who has polluted it. (91:7-10)

وَ قُلِ الْحَقُّ مِنْ رَّبِّكُمْ ۚ فَمَنْ شَآءَ فَلْيُؤْمِنْ وَّ مَنْ شَآءَ فَلْيَكْفُرْ ۚ

(Tell them) That this is the Truth from your Lord. So, whoever wishes can believe in it, and whoever wishes can reject it. (18:29)

Q & A and Discussion

Chapter 7

Punishment for Blasphemy

This chapter discusses another controversial topic in Islam: the punishment for blasphemy, which has been criticized heavily even by a minority of Islamic scholars.

Punishment for Blasphemy

Introduction

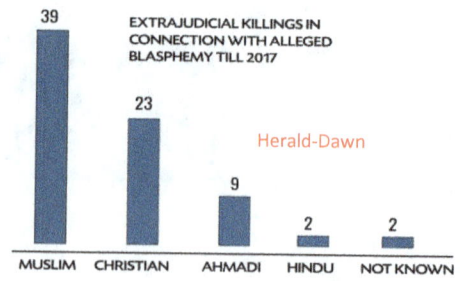

- On 14 February 1989, Iran's supreme leader issued a fatwa ordering Muslims to execute author Salman Rushdie over the publication of The Satanic Verses.
- It was quite an unfamiliar concept at that time, but since then, laws have been implemented in many Islamic countries suggesting the death penalty for the blasphemer (especially against Prophet Muhammad (PBUH)).
- The relatively recent controversy of depicting Prophet Muhammad (PBUH) also resulted in many violent and fatal incidents in many Muslim and non-Muslim countries.
- It is generally accepted that no civilized society should defile religious personalities, let alone Prophets, but in a broader framework, this friction will continue to exist between the West's wrongly perceived. commitment to free speech and Muslim's extreme reaction to blasphemy
- The most significant aspect of this law of blasphemy is the extrajudicial killings in connection with alleged blasphemy in some parts of the world
- Muslims must realize that they are not helping their religion by responding to criticism or even mockery with violence and rage.

General Understanding

- Most of the religious literature and extreme forms of blasphemy laws implemented in some of the Muslim countries suggest that the person who commits blasphemy must be executed.
- The accused is not allowed to repent or provide any explanation.
- If enough people testify against the accused, the accused can be prosecuted in court.
- The law does not consider the religion of the accused, and the punishment is implemented for both Muslims and non-Muslims.
- It is generally observed that the extreme position taken in this matter is because a good number of religious scholars insist on killing the blasphemer, and it is usually considered a bargain between the ruling and religious classes.

Classical vs Contemporary Scholarship

Classical Scholars

- Traditionally, the Jurists of Islam do not consider it a separate crime and suggest the death penalty for the following reasons:
  - Due to blasphemy, this person has already left Islam and should be executed for apostasy, as per the law of apostasy (according to their understanding).
  - If that person is a non-Muslim, then due to breaching of the contract between a Muslim state and the *Dhimmis* (protected minority) under which the Muslim state protected him, and as a result of this crime, that protection has been taken away, so the person must be killed.
- In summary, traditional scholars have not suggested any punishment for blasphemy.

Contemporary Position

- In modern times, there are three primary sources presented in this regard when laws are made for the punishment of blasphemy:
  - Verses of Surah Maidah 33-34, which describe the punishment for a person who creates disorder in the land (it will be discussed later).
  - Scattered incidents that are reported in the lifetime of the Prophet.
  - This weak hadith appeared at the end of the 3rd century AH.

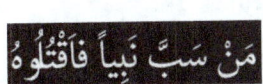 

Hussain bin Ali reported from his father that the Prophet said: "Whoever dishonors the Prophets must be killed, and whoever curses my companions must be lashed.
(Al Mujam Al Kabeer Tabarani # 235)

How to approach this issue?

- In order to understand the problem in its entirety, there are multiple issues that we should look at:

  1 Has the Quran, Sunnah, or even scholars of Islam ever prescribed punishment for blasphemy?

  2 Can the death penalty be the punishment for blasphemy?

  3 Should there be laws to tackle blasphemy?

Punishment for Blasphemy in Quran & Sunnah

- The Quran or Sunnah does not mention any punishment for blasphemy in the Shariah.

- The prescribed punishment for blasphemy, as suggested in recent times, has no basis in the Quran and Sunnah, and even in any of the authentic narrations attributed to Prophet Muhammad.

- It is important to note that the Quran has mentioned various incidents in which Quraysh, hypocrites, and People of the Book had either insulted the Prophet (and it quoted them) or had the intention to insult him, but still, it does not talk about any worldly punishment for them.

فَاصْدَعْ بِمَا تُؤْمَرُ وَ اَعْرِضْ عَنِ الْمُشْرِكِيْنَ ۚ اِنَّا كَفَيْنٰكَ الْمُسْتَهْزِءِيْنَ

So, (O Muhammad), announce what has been commanded to you, and disregard these Idolators. We are sufficient to handle these mockers on your behalf. (15:94-95)

وَ لَا تَسُبُّوا الَّذِيْنَ يَدْعُوْنَ مِنْ دُوْنِ اللّٰهِ فَيَسُبُّوا اللّٰهَ عَدْوًا بِغَيْرِ عِلْمٍ

Do not curse those whom they call other than God, lest they start cursing Allah without realizing it. (6:108)

وَ قَدْ نَزَّلَ عَلَيْكُمْ فِى الْكِتٰبِ اَنْ اِذَا سَمِعْتُمْ اٰيٰتِ اللّٰهِ يُكْفَرُ بِهَا وَ يُسْتَهْزَاُ بِهَا فَلَا تَقْعُدُوْا مَعَهُمْ حَتّٰى يَخُوْضُوْا فِىْ حَدِيْثٍ غَيْرِهٖۤ ۖ اِنَّكُمْ اِذًا مِّثْلُهُمْ ۗ اِنَّ اللّٰهَ جَامِعُ الْمُنٰفِقِيْنَ وَ الْكٰفِرِيْنَ فِىْ جَهَنَّمَ جَمِيْعًا

And it has already been revealed to you in this Book that when you hear that the verses of Allah are being denied [by them] and ridiculed, do not sit with them until they move to another conversation. Otherwise, you would then be like them. Indeed, Allah will gather the hypocrites and disbelievers in Hellfire altogether. (4:140)

- These were all good occasions where Allah could have mentioned any worldly punishment for this heinous act. There is no doubt about the severity of this evil act, but Allah only talked about the punishment in the Hereafter in response to their mocking. In the end, the disbelievers were punished for rejecting the message and its messenger, as per the law of God.

Apostasy Argument

- As stated earlier, classical scholars do not consider blasphemy a separate crime and never prescribe punishment for it. For them, the accused must be executed under the Law of Apostasy and the Law of Dhimmis.
- Even if we assume that there is a death penalty for apostasy and the non-Muslims are still Dhimmis (protected minority), the Muslim Jurists agree that:
  1. The apostate/dhimmi must be given time and opportunity to think about what he has done or said.
  2. The verdict must be based solely on the statement given by the accused.
- The blasphemy laws in place today do not address **any of these provisions**, suggesting that they are not even compliant with the rulings of traditional Islamic jurisprudence.
- The rulings of the classical jurists suggest:

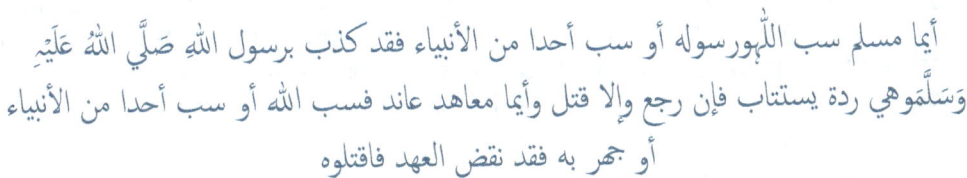

A Muslim who blasphemes against God, the Prophet, or any of God's messengers is guilty of denying the Prophet (PBUH). This is apostasy, which entails that repentance is demanded of the offender. If he repents, he shall be released; if not, he shall be killed. Similarly, if anyone from amongst non-Muslims protected under the pact becomes hostile by openly blaspheming against God or the Prophet (PBUH) or any of God's messengers, he is guilty of violating the pact; you shall kill him, too.

[Abu Abdullah Muhammad ibn Abi Bakr ibn Qayyim, Zad al-ma'ad fi hadyi khayr al-'ibad, 1st ed., vol. 4 (Beirut: Dar al-kutub al-'ilmiyyah, 1998), 379.]

Events in the lifetime of Prophet used as a basis

- Analyzing all the scattered events* from the Seerah of the Prophet, it is clear that the disbelievers or hypocrites who were killed committed the crime of treason or disorder supporting enemies against Muslims, after the punishment of death from God was already announced for them.
- Secondly, events cannot be the source for laws, as the entire context, reasoning, situation, and many such factors are missing from the reports.
- Most scholars agree that the Quran and Sunnah alone can be the source of law in Shariah.
- Some events in the Prophet's lifetime suggest otherwise, as he forgave many people for this act.

  * Please read "*Maqamat*" from Javed Ahmed Ghamidi for more details

Death Penalty for Blasphemy

- The Quran has prescribed the death penalty as the extreme punishment for two crimes only:
    1. Intentional Murder. (2:178-179)
    2. Anarchy or disorder in the land against people's lives, wealth, and honor. (5:33-34)

اِنَّمَا جَزٰٓؤُا الَّذِيْنَ يُحَارِبُوْنَ اللّٰهَ وَ رَسُوْلَهٗ وَ يَسْعَوْنَ فِي الْاَرْضِ فَسَادًا اَنْ يُّقَتَّلُوْۤا اَوْ يُصَلَّبُوْۤا اَوْ تُقَطَّعَ اَيْدِيْهِمْ وَ اَرْجُلُهُمْ مِّنْ خِلَافٍ اَوْ يُنْفَوْا مِنَ الْاَرْضِ ذٰلِكَ لَهُمْ خِزْيٌ فِي الدُّنْيَا وَ لَهُمْ فِي الْاٰخِرَةِ عَذَابٌ عَظِيْمٌ اِلَّا الَّذِيْنَ تَابُوْا مِنْ قَبْلِ اَنْ تَقْدِرُوْا عَلَيْهِمْ فَاعْلَمُوْۤا اَنَّ اللّٰهَ غَفُوْرٌ رَّحِيْمٌ

The punishment for those who fight against God and His Prophet to create disorder in the land is that they are executed exemplary, be crucified, have their hands and feet cut off from opposite sides, or be exiled. This disgrace is theirs in the world, and in the Hereafter, they shall have severe retribution, except those who repent before you overpower them (so do not exceed in severity). Know well that God is Oft-Forgiving, Ever-Merciful. (5:33-34)

- These punishments (the death penalty is the extreme) can be given only if the offender persists in blasphemy defiantly and resorts to disorder in the land despite repeated warnings.
- The directive does not apply to those who submit and repent before authorities apprehend them.
- The context and directives given in these verses indicate that these punishments can only be implemented after these three things have occurred:
    1. The accused has been allowed to explain and repent.
    2. The case will be filed against him only after he refuses to repent and insists on his stance.
    3. The death penalty is not mandatory. The court can determine the degree of leniency based on the nature of the offense and the offender's circumstances.
- The current law in some countries imposes these sentences solely on the basis of testimony, without regard to the accused's confession or denial.
- If the law is based on these verses, then some of the critical legal aspects have been ignored, as stipulated by these verses.

Should there be Laws for Blasphemy?

- There is no doubt that insulting the Prophets or any religious figure to whom people have an emotional or religious attachment is a crime and must not go unpunished legally.
- Laws can be made keeping in view the overall situation of Muslims in the land or globally that serve the purpose of their betterment and avoiding disorder and hatred in society.
- An Islamic state is free to make laws outside of the realm of Shariah, depending on its situation.
- However, when making such laws, it is incumbent upon the Islamic State not to violate the directives of Shariah, which has limited the death penalty to only two types of crimes.

What else should be done against blasphemy?

- Both Muslims and non-Muslims visiting a Muslim land must be adequately educated and informed about the position of Prophet Muhammad in the eyes of the Muslims and the sensitivities associated with his persona.
- The cultural and value divide between East and the West demands that Muslim states should raise the issue of blasphemy in international forums and explain why cultural attitudes should not cross religious boundaries.
- To gain global acceptability, the Muslim states should remove the extreme elements and behavior from these laws.
- Our scholars must come out and condemn in the strongest terms the acts of mob justice conducted in the name of these laws, and educate common Muslims about it.
- The laws must be amended to focus on the accused's statement rather than on the testimony of the people, to prevent misuse of these laws.
- We must create an environment of general education about the life and character of Prophet Muhammad, so that more people come to know the true personality of our beloved Prophet.

Q & A and Discussion

Chapter 8

Homosexuality and the LGBTQ+ community

This chapter discusses a very sensitive topic that did not come to light until the late 20th or early 21st century, and many people are confused about Islam's position on it.

Homosexuality and the LGBTQ+ community

Introduction

- Homosexuality, a term coined in the late 19th century, refers to sexual interest in and attraction to members of one's sex – the term gay is often used as a synonym for homosexual.
- The references to same-sex relationships can be found in the literature of ancient Greece and ancient Rome.
- Homosexual behavior has received a variety of treatments at different times and in different cultures, from approved to tolerated to banned and punished.
- In Abrahamic traditions, it is considered sinful, but many Jurists also considered it punishable by law.
- Due to increased political activism and international human rights campaigns, the attitude towards homosexuality and homosexuals is changing fast in more and more countries.
- There are conflicting views about the reasons for homosexuality: abnormal human behavior, psychologically deviant behavior, genetic issues, medical conditions, sexual perversion, lifestyle choice, etc.
- This is transforming into an LGBTQ community, which is a loosely defined grouping of sexual orientations outside of what's considered normal.

Homosexuality is not a new phenomenon

While it's a common misconception that non-heteronormative relationships are a modern invention, they are actually a deeply rooted part of human history found across nearly every culture and era. From the sacred bands of Ancient Greece to the "two-spirit" traditions in many Indigenous American societies, same-sex bonds have existed for millennia, often integrated into the social or religious fabric. The current sense of "newness" is largely a byproduct of increased visibility; the digital age and social media have simply provided a global platform for identities that were previously suppressed, marginalized, or erased from historical records.

Islam's Position on Homosexuality

وَ الَّذِيْنَ هُمْ لِفُرُوْجِهِمْ حٰفِظُوْنَ ۙ اِلَّا عَلٰۤى اَزْوَاجِهِمْ اَوْ مَا مَلَكَتْ اَيْمَانُهُمْ فَاِنَّهُمْ غَيْرُ مَلُوْمِيْنَ

فَمَنِ ابْتَغٰى وَرَآءَ ذٰلِكَ فَاُولٰٓئِكَ هُمُ الْعٰدُوْنَ

And those who guard their private parts, except their wives and/or from what 'their right hands possess' because in this matter, there is no blame on them. But whoever wishes besides that would be from the transgressors. (Surah Maarij:30-31)

- Purification is the objective of all the commandments given in Shariah.
- The Shariah prohibits all sexual relationships outside of marriage (other than with slave women, which was tolerated due to long-held custom in Arabian society).
- Historically, regardless of religion and society, marriage has always been considered a union between **a man and a woman**, and Islam considers homosexuality a danger to this institution.
- Quran, through the story of the People of Lot, has given the verdict that God considers same-sex relationships a grave sin and a severe deviation from the nature in which human beings are created.
- There is no specific punishment prescribed in Shariah for this act, as this does not come within the definition of Zina (adultery), although there is a difference of opinion among scholars.

Quran on Homosexuality

- The Quran's position on homosexual relationships is very clear from its statements and the dialogue between Prophet Lut and his nation. In these verses, the Quran is specific about male-male relationships, but one can conclude that it also applies to female-female relationships.

وَ لُوْطًا اِذْ قَالَ لِقَوْمِهٖۤ اَتَأْتُوْنَ الْفَاحِشَةَ مَا سَبَقَكُمْ بِهَا مِنْ اَحَدٍ مِّنَ الْعٰلَمِيْنَ

اِنَّكُمْ لَتَأْتُوْنَ الرِّجَالَ شَهْوَةً مِّنْ دُوْنِ النِّسَآءِ ؕ بَلْ اَنْتُمْ قَوْمٌ مُّسْرِفُوْنَ

وَ مَا كَانَ جَوَابَ قَوْمِهٖۤ اِلَّاۤ اَنْ قَالُوْۤا اَخْرِجُوْهُمْ مِّنْ قَرْيَتِكُمْ ۚ اِنَّهُمْ اُنَاسٌ يَّتَطَهَّرُوْنَ

فَاَنْجَيْنٰهُ وَ اَهْلَهٗۤ اِلَّا امْرَاَتَهٗ ۖ كَانَتْ مِنَ الْغٰبِرِيْنَ وَ اَمْطَرْنَا عَلَيْهِمْ مَّطَرًا ؕ فَانْظُرْ كَيْفَ كَانَ عَاقِبَةُ الْمُجْرِمِيْنَ

And (We sent) Lut, when he said to his people: What! Do you commit this vulgarity that no one in the world has committed before you (as a society)? So, you fulfill your lust with males besides females; You are definitely a person who has transgressed. But the response of his people was nothing but saying, 'Throw them out of your town; they are trying to show themselves as a purified people.' So, We saved him and his followers, except his wife; she was one of those who remained behind. And We rained upon them a rain (of stones) the way it should be rained (on them); Then see what happened with those criminals. (7:80-84)

How to deal with the LGBTQ Community?

- More and more people who associate themselves with the LGBTQ community are 'coming out' (regardless of the reasons for their inclinations) and sharing their identity openly with others in the society around them – this was not the case before.

- This 'identity' has become a community to safeguard their rights and to become a voice in society.

- It is often observed that people who are religious in their upbringing feel awkward just by knowing that someone in their friends or relatives belongs to this community – sometimes young adults come under immense pressure from their families not to befriend 'such' people.

- Whether we agree with the reasons for such inclinations, we must accept the fact that it is OK to have a difference of opinion about sexual orientation, like in any other matter, and we must learn how to live in a society with such differences.

- Our attitude towards people of the LGBTQ community should be no different than what we display to any other member of society (as a neighbor, friend, relative, fellow citizen, etc.), while maintaining a completely different stance on this issue (similar to issues like consuming alcohol).

- If they are a close friend or relative of yours, then use this opportunity to discuss this matter with them privately or through counseling and present your opinion and arguments in a respectful manner.

- Looking down upon them or ostracizing them would be considered a discriminatory act towards our fellow human beings, merely based on their sexual orientation (which, anyway, is a private matter). Also, it will not resolve this difference, and you will lose an opportunity to keep someone engaged in this matter, knowing that Allah does not want anyone to get involved in this sin.

Hate Crimes

- In the wake of a few shooting incidents in different parts of the world, including the US, there is a view circulating that Islam preaches violence toward the LGBTQ community.

- The Story of the People of Lut by no means teaches us that as Muslims, we have the right to belittle, hate, or dehumanize other fellow beings who choose to have different moral values than ours.
- This negative attitude among many religious-minded people towards the LGBTQ community has created the problem of homophobia, which people use as a justification for targeting LGBTQ members as less than human.

Remember

- The sanctity of human life is above and beyond any difference of opinion and must be upheld at all costs.
- This is God-given freedom they are exercising as human beings; let Him be the Judge.
- Hate the sin, not the sinner.

Advice to the LGBTQ Members

- God created this life to test us, and everyone in the world is going through many tests.
- As part of this scheme of tests, we are given many challenges: emotions, desires, free will, illnesses, disabilities, etc.
- Through these tests, God intends to select people from this world who have led a life of purity (in food, body, and morals) for eternal comfort and the pleasures of the next life in His Paradise.
- The test is how we use our God-given knowledge, intellect, and moral sense to purify ourselves amid these challenges.
- God demands this purity in all aspects of our lives, but mostly in our private lives, which includes our sexual lives also.
- God has already directed us towards the natural and the purest way of fulfilling our sexual needs with our wives – any other way is considered impure.
- Sexual activities between two males or two females are considered an unnatural and impure way of satisfying one's needs and hence prohibited in the Shariah of Islam.
- Even with our wives, anal sex is prohibited, as it is also against the objective of purity.
- God demands our best efforts, made with sincerity, to achieve the purity that will qualify us for His eternal pleasures.

How to Address the Problem

- There can be a couple of main reasons for the deviation from 'natural' sexual orientation (for gays and lesbians):
  - Psychological reasons due to the environment, life experiences, influenced by certain ideologies, etc.
  - Biological disorder at the time of birth or due to the use of some medications.
- God has asked us to make every effort and take all necessary steps to address the problem, including, but not limited to, talking to a psychologist and other medical specialists.
- In the case of transgender individuals, if the person's gender can be defined (medically) and he/she can marry the opposite gender, they can marry. But if they are not able to perform normal sexual acts, then they must stay unmarried and consider it a massive test from God for which they will be rewarded immensely.
- Make Dua to God as He controls everything in this world.

Natural inclination vs 'lifestyle' choice

- All humans are born with a *fitrah*—a natural inclination toward that which is divinely ordained. Within this framework, heterosexuality is viewed as the natural state. Adopting a same-sex identity as a "lifestyle" is often seen as a departure from this natural state, influenced by social normalization or cultural trends rather than biological necessity.
- A critical distinction in Islam is between a person's inner feelings and their outward actions. Having same-sex attractions is not considered a sin in itself, as these urges are often seen as beyond a person's control. Instead, the test for a believer lies in their ability to refrain from acting on these desires.
- For those who experience same-sex attraction without any underlying medical or psychological cause, Islam's view is that this serves as a trial from Allah. Choosing to live according to Islamic sexual ethics (limiting sexual relations to a marriage between a man and a woman) is viewed as a form of worship and self-restraint (*also called Jihad with Nafs*).
- There is a strong rejection within most Islamic communities of the idea that homosexuality should be normalized as a valid "lifestyle choice" or identity. This perspective argues that while individuals should be treated with compassion, the public promotion or justification of same-sex acts contradicts clear Quranic prohibitions and undermines the traditional family structure.

Q & A and Discussion

Chapter 9

"Hijab" or Women's Veil

This chapter discusses the topic of hijab that has been used by non-Muslims in the West to show that Islam is a repressive religion towards women.

"Hijab" or Women's veil

Introduction

View of a Muslim Woman   View of the West

- The word "hijab" is not used in the Quran or Ahadith for modest clothing or wearing a headscarf as we use it today for women – it is used for a physical barrier that God exclusively asked the wives of the Prophet to maintain between them and non-related men when talking to them in their houses.

- These instructions were given to the wives of the Prophet due to the mischievous attitude adopted by the enemies of Islam in the later part of the Medinan life of Prophet Muhammad.

- The contemporary usage of this word is now reduced to "wearing a headscarf" by a Muslim woman.

- There is a difference of opinion among the Jurists about what is considered "hijab" as per the instructions of the Quran, but everyone agrees that it is a symbol of modesty and dignity adopted by the faithful female followers of Islam.

- The main controversy in the context of "hijab" is about the face covering, which is also known as the veil or "niqab" – some scholars consider "niqab" as mandatory and part of "hijab".

- In the West, some people look at the "hijab" as a sign of oppression of Muslim women.

- Muslim women in the West have been wearing it to identify themselves as Muslims and as a sign of modesty, but with growing Islamophobia now, they feel fear and anxiety about being visible and identifiable in public.

- The majority of Muslim women acquire hijab by choice and are not forced; however, it may not be the situation in some of the Eastern cultures where women are forced to wear it.

The true purpose of 'hijab'

- Before we delve into the scholarly debate on the matter and what Islam says about it, let's first look into what Islam wants from this.
- In Islam, the hijab is far more than a physical head covering; it is a holistic manifestation of *Haya* (modesty and shyness), which is considered the very signature trait of the faith for both men and women.
- Linguistically, the word Haya is derived from Hayat (life), suggesting that a person's spiritual vitality is directly proportionate to their sense of modesty; to lose one's Haya is, in a sense, to be spiritually dead.
- The real essence of hijab is an outer reflection of an inner commitment to God-consciousness (Taqwa). It functions as a metaphysical and ethical barrier that governs not only attire but also speech, behavior, and even one's presence on social media.
- By practicing hijab, a believer seeks to be recognized for their character and intellect rather than their physical appearance, essentially reclaiming their identity from societal beauty standards and dedicating it solely to the pleasure of Allah.

The more 'conservative' view on veil

- Even though there is a difference of opinion among scholars about what is covered in the concept of "Hijab," the following views are prevalent among the majority of the traditional scholars of Islam and practiced in many Muslim societies (although it is not practiced as much as it was before):
  - The women must cover their entire body from head to toe except for their face, hands, and feet when coming in front of non-mahram (with whom marriage is permissible) men. Some scholars include a face covering in "hijab".
  - According to this opinion, the directives related to "hijab" are given in Surah Nur, verses 30-31, Surah Ahzab, verses 58-61, 53-55, and 32-33.
  - Women should not come in front of non-mahram men, including relatives, unnecessarily unless it is required for a genuine reason.
  - The women should not speak in front of non-mahram men (hijab of voice) unless it is necessary.
  - The best place for them is their homes – they should avoid leaving them unnecessarily.
  - They cannot leave the house alone without a male relative accompanying them.
  - They should not wear such perfume whose fragrance can be smelled from a distance.

Understanding from the Quran

- This topic came in the Quran at three different places. We will explore all three places of the Quran and understand what Allah wants from Muslims in this matter.

General Directives (Surah Nur 30-31)

- General directives were given to Muslim men and women on how to interact and behave with one another to purify their hearts. These are the etiquette for gender interaction that should always be followed, regardless of time or place.

Special Circumstances (Surah Ahzab 58-61)

- In those times, Muslim women were given specific instructions to protect themselves from troublemakers in situations and places where they felt insecure and harassed. Similar preventive measures can be adopted today if the situation demands.

Special instructions to the wives of the Prophet (Surah Ahzab 32-33, 53-55)

- Specific instructions given to the wives of the Prophet due to their special status, which do not apply to other common Muslim women.

Etiquette of Gender Interaction

- Since the word 'hijab' is not used in the Quran for the topic under discussion, it is important to note that it is better to say that Allah provided the etiquette of gender interaction in Surah Nur. Verses 30-31 from Surah Nur sum up the norms and etiquette of gender interaction.
- The objective of these instructions is to attain the purity of the hearts (the objective of all directives).
- When friends, relatives, and acquaintances visit each other, where both men and women will be present, we are asked to follow certain etiquette:
- Both should restrain their gazes – look at each other as decent people do when talking. Having modesty in our gazes does not mean that we should not look at each other, but instead we should not look at each other with sexual desire.
- Both should 'guard' their private parts by dressing appropriately – this is not to cover but to cover in such a way that it does not reveal those parts in any shape or form (extended clothing is preferred).
- A woman's chest is considered a private part, and appropriate dress should be worn that does not reveal it in any way.

- Women who have worn embellishments should not be displayed except before the innermost circle (list given in verse 31). Especially when this embellishment is near the woman's chest, it must be covered. This does not include embellishments on other exposed body parts (such as hands, face, and feet).
- That jewelry that makes a sound (quite common in the eastern part of the world) is allowed, but no deliberate effort should be made to produce more sound, which may attract men's attention (this was a common practice among Arab women).

قُلْ لِّلْمُؤْمِنِيْنَ يَغُضُّوْا مِنْ اَبْصَارِهِمْ وَ يَحْفَظُوْا فُرُوْجَهُمْ ۚ ذٰلِكَ اَزْكٰى لَهُمْ ؕ اِنَّ اللّٰهَ خَبِيْرٌ بِمَا يَصْنَعُوْنَ

وَ قُلْ لِّلْمُؤْمِنٰتِ يَغْضُضْنَ مِنْ اَبْصَارِهِنَّ وَ يَحْفَظْنَ فُرُوْجَهُنَّ وَ لَا يُبْدِيْنَ زِيْنَتَهُنَّ اِلَّا مَا ظَهَرَ مِنْهَا وَ لْيَضْرِبْنَ

بِخُمُرِهِنَّ عَلٰى جُيُوْبِهِنَّ ۪ وَ لَا يُبْدِيْنَ زِيْنَتَهُنَّ اِلَّا لِبُعُوْلَتِهِنَّ اَوْ اٰبَآئِهِنَّ اَوْ اٰبَآءِ بُعُوْلَتِهِنَّ اَوْ اَبْنَآئِهِنَّ اَوْ اَبْنَآءِ بُعُوْلَتِهِنَّ اَوْ

اِخْوَانِهِنَّ اَوْ بَنِيْ اِخْوَانِهِنَّ اَوْ بَنِيْ اَخَوٰتِهِنَّ اَوْ نِسَآئِهِنَّ اَوْ مَا مَلَكَتْ اَيْمَانُهُنَّ اَوِ التّٰبِعِيْنَ غَيْرِ اُولِى الْاِرْبَةِ مِنَ الرِّجَالِ

اَوِ الطِّفْلِ الَّذِيْنَ لَمْ يَظْهَرُوْا عَلٰى عَوْرٰتِ النِّسَآءِ ۪ وَ لَا يَضْرِبْنَ بِاَرْجُلِهِنَّ لِيُعْلَمَ مَا يُخْفِيْنَ مِنْ زِيْنَتِهِنَّ ؕ وَ تُوْبُوْا اِلَى

اللّٰهِ جَمِيْعًا اَيُّهَ الْمُؤْمِنُوْنَ لَعَلَّكُمْ تُفْلِحُوْنَ

Tell believing men to restrain their eyes and guard their private parts [if women are present in these houses]. That is purer for them. And indeed, Allah is well aware of what they do. And tell the believing women to restrain their eyes, guard their private parts, display their ornaments only those which are normally revealed, and draw their coverings over their bosoms. And they should not reveal their embellishments to anyone save their husbands or their fathers or their husbands' fathers or their sons or their husbands' sons or their brothers or their brothers' sons or their sisters' sons or other women of acquaintance or their slaves or the subservient male servants who are not attracted to women or children who have no awareness of the hidden aspects of women. And they should [also] not stamp their feet to draw attention to their hidden ornaments. Believers! Turn to Allah in repentance that you may prosper. (Surah Nur 30-31)

Verses of Surah Ahzab 58-61 (special circumstances)

- God gave some specific instructions about a special circumstance.
- Some miscreants started a smear campaign against the family of Prophet Muhammad and other Muslim women.
- God instructed Muslim women to wrap (draw forward) any of the shawls they have over them, to cover them fully when they go out to insecure places.
- Such attire would distinguish them from women of lewd character, and they would not be teased on the pretext of being outwardly like such women.
- It is evident from the statement "so that they be distinguished [from other women] and not be harassed" that the instructions given here are for a specific situation and not general.

Instructions to the Wives of the Prophet (32-33, 53-55)

- These instructions did not apply to common Muslim women.
- They should not be kind and affectionate in their speech to everyone.
- They must speak in clear and simple/flat tones.
- They should remain in their homes.
- If they must go out, they should not display their ornaments and finery.
- Anyone who wants something from their private places must ask for it from behind a veil (called Hijab in the verse).

The difference of opinion

- The difference of opinion among scholars on this matter stems from the fact that some traditional scholars considered all three sections of the Quran (discussed previously) to be the general directives regarding women's attire and their dealings with others.
- As can be understood from reading these verses, the verses of Surah Ahzab (58-61 and 32-33 / 53-55) are not meant for all women in all circumstances.
- The general directives for men and women when interacting with each other are explicitly given in the verses of Surah Nur.
- The argument presented by the scholars who follow such opinion is that since we are living in a morally degraded society, the directives of the Quran mentioned in Surah Ahzab are applicable, and women must follow them.

Niqab – The Face Veil

- Some recent scholars of Islam think that, due to the instructions given in verses 58-61, women must cover their faces (called Niqab) as part of the "hijab" when meeting with non-mahram males or going out in public.
- None of the classical scholars considered face-covering mandatory.
- Verses 58-61 of Surah Ahzab talk about a particular situation in which Muslim women were advised to put a loose sheet of cloth on themselves to cover themselves (including their faces) to avoid being victimized by the hypocrites and miscreants of the society.
- There are scores of narrations from the time of the Prophet Muhammad that suggest women did not cover their faces then, as the Prophet used to recognize them.

- Ummul Momineen Aisha (RA) reported that women of Medinah used to come to pray Fajr in the mosque, and the Prophet used to pray Fajr so early that it was hard to recognize them by their faces in the darkness.
- The main argument presented by the proponents of the Niqab is that since Muslim women are living in a similar unsafe situation at this time as it was in Medina, it is necessary to wear a Niqab as the directives were meant in general for such circumstances.

Q & A and Discussion

Chapter 10

Dating or falling in "love"

This chapter discusses a topic that is new to Muslim society, and Muslim scholars are addressing it in accordance with the guidance provided by the Quran and Sunnah.

Dating or Falling in "Love"

Introduction

- The definition of "dating" differs across cultures, even within Western societies—it began as 'chaperone courtship.'
- Regardless of these differences, each party aims to assess the other's suitability as a partner in an intimate relationship or as a future spouse.
- Dating, as it is currently practiced in much of Western society, never existed openly in the Muslim world or in Muslim cultures.
- The attraction between men and women is natural and forms the basis of any relationship, including marriage.
- The young Muslim men and women growing up in Western societies find themselves confused and in a peculiar situation, attracted towards different versions of dating like 'halal dating':
  - feeling the pressure of society.
  - challenges in finding a marriage partner.
  - mentally and psychologically, they cannot accept the concept of 'arranged marriage.'
  - don't know exactly what the limit their religion has imposed on them is in this matter.

Dating in the West

From a purely cultural perspective, the concept of "dating" as we know it today is a surprisingly recent invention, tracing back only about 100 to 130 years in Western societies like the United States. Before the 20th century, the dominant cultural practice was "calling." A man would visit a woman at her home, sitting in her family's parlor under a chaperone's watchful eye. The rise of urbanization and the mass production of automobiles in the 1920s shifted this ritual from the private home to public spaces such as movie theaters and dance halls, giving youth unprecedented "privacy and freedom". (Source: Internet)

Basic Principles

- Before getting into the topic of Islam's position on this, let's first understand some basic principles on which this matter rests.

1- Protecting the Institution of Family

وَ الَّذِينَ هُمْ لِفُرُوجِهِمْ حَافِظُونَ ۚ إِلَّا عَلَىٰ أَزْوَاجِهِمْ أَوْ مَا مَلَكَتْ أَيْمَانُهُمْ فَإِنَّهُمْ غَيْرُ مَلُومِينَ

فَمَنِ ابْتَغَىٰ وَرَآءَ ذَٰلِكَ فَأُولَٰئِكَ هُمُ الْعَادُونَ

And those who guard their private parts, except their wives and/or from what 'their right hands possess' because in this matter, there is no blame on them. But whoever wishes besides that would be from the transgressors. (Surah Maarij:30-31)

- The family is the nucleus of civilization and the basic unit of society, and it is an important aspect of Islam's social concept.
- In the eyes of God, the welfare of the child is the most important aspect of this unit of family.
- God wants to protect this unit of the family from all those dangers that can jeopardize the survival of this unit and hence restrict the sexual relationship between husband and wife.

2 - Illicit Relationships are Forbidden

وَ لَا تَقْرَبُوا الزِّنَىٰ ۖ إِنَّهُ كَانَ فَاحِشَةً ۖ وَ سَآءَ سَبِيلًا

You shall not draw near to adultery, for it is lewd, and its way is evil." (Surah Israa:32)

- The family is founded on a sacred, pure relationship, and this is only possible when there is no illicit relationship between a man and a woman before or after marriage.
- To make sure that the sexual relationship is limited to husband and wife, God declared any illicit relationship outside of marriage as prohibited.
- God wants to save society from becoming one where sexual relations are taken casually and morally bankrupt.

3 - Etiquettes of Gender Interaction

- The Quran discusses the etiquette of gender interaction in Surah Nur, which also directly addresses this topic.
- These verses from Surah Nur sum up the norms and etiquette of gender interaction. We are asked to adhere to these norms to avoid getting into the traps of Satan. The objective of these instructions is to attain the purity of the heart.

وَ قُلْ لِّلْمُؤْمِنِينَ يَغُضُّوا مِنْ اَبْصَارِهِمْ وَ يَحْفَظُوا فُرُوجَهُمْ ذٰلِكَ اَزْكٰى لَهُمْ اِنَّ اللهَ خَبِيرٌ بِمَا يَصْنَعُونَ

لِّلْمُؤْمِنٰتِ يَغْضُضْنَ مِنْ اَبْصَارِهِنَّ وَ يَحْفَظْنَ فُرُوجَهُنَّ وَ لَا يُبْدِينَ زِينَتَهُنَّ اِلَّا مَا ظَهَرَ مِنْهَا وَ لْيَضْرِبْنَ بِخُمُرِهِنَّ

عَلٰى جُيُوبِهِنَّ وَ لَا يُبْدِينَ زِينَتَهُنَّ اِلَّا لِبُعُولَتِهِنَّ اَوْ اٰبَائِهِنَّ اَوْ اٰبَاءِ بُعُولَتِهِنَّ اَوْ اَبْنَائِهِنَّ اَوْ اَبْنَاءِ بُعُولَتِهِنَّ اَوْ

اِخْوَانِهِنَّ اَوْ بَنِي اِخْوَانِهِنَّ اَوْ بَنِي اَخَوٰتِهِنَّ اَوْ نِسَائِهِنَّ اَوْ مَا مَلَكَتْ اَيْمَانُهُنَّ اَوِ التّٰبِعِينَ غَيْرِ اُولِي الْاِرْبَةِ مِنَ

الرِّجَالِ اَوِ الطِّفْلِ الَّذِينَ لَمْ يَظْهَرُوا عَلٰى عَوْرٰتِ النِّسَاءِ وَ لَا يَضْرِبْنَ بِاَرْجُلِهِنَّ لِيُعْلَمَ مَا يُخْفِينَ مِنْ زِينَتِهِنَّ وَ

تُوبُوا اِلَى اللهِ جَمِيعًا اَيُّهَ الْمُؤْمِنُونَ لَعَلَّكُمْ تُفْلِحُونَ

Tell believing men to restrain their eyes and guard their private parts [if there are women present in these houses]. That is purer for them. And indeed, Allah is well aware of what they do. And tell the believing women to restrain their eyes and guard their private parts to display their ornaments only those which are typically revealed and to draw their coverings over their bosoms. And they should not reveal their embellishments to anyone save their husbands or their fathers or their husbands' fathers or their sons or their husbands' sons or their brothers or their brothers' sons or their sisters' sons or other women of acquaintance or their slaves or the subservient male servants who are not attracted to women or children who have no awareness of the hidden aspects of women. And they should [also] not stamp their feet to draw attention to their hidden ornaments. Believers! Turn to Allah in repentance that you may prosper. (Surah Nur: 30-31)

Islam's Position on dating and love

- Going back to the principles outlined in the previous pages, if a man and a woman can guard the limits set forth by God in these verses, then Islam does not prohibit them from falling in "love" with each other or finding a way to get to know each other before marriage.

- This is also true of friendships between people of opposite genders at any stage of life.

- However, since we are weak in controlling our sexual instincts, God, our Creator, has instructed us to "not go near adultery," which includes any steps that could lead us to what has been prohibited.

- Always remember that the goal of the etiquette of gender interaction given by our Creator is to keep us outside of the gravitational field of Zina, which is at the core of the prohibition and is considered one of the major sins in Islam after shirk and murder.

- God took one step further when it comes to Zina and made it a crime, as it is a crime against society, which results in its moral deterioration (the evidence of this is in front of us).

- God related the instructions to the purity of the hearts, which is always at the center of all instructions given in our Shariah.

Few Key Points

- The habit of going into temporary relationships (as we see in Western society) without having the goal of finding a partner for marriage easily turns into an addiction that will continue to raise its head even after the marriage, destroying the marital life.

- The longer the 'friendship', the greater the chance that people will cross the boundaries of the Shariah.

- Younger people often think that they are in full control of their emotions, but these are the deceptive thoughts of Satan – even Prophets of God are not saved from these emotions, only Allah saved them (as per Surah Yusuf).

- When people meet in a limited setting before marriage, they are likely to pretend to be what they are not, leading to incorrect judgments and decisions.

- Dating, especially in the form of secret relationships, often damages the couple's reputation and destroys their future marital life.

- Dating has not proven to be the solution for finding a good spouse who leads to a blissful marriage, because the divorce rate in Western societies is much higher than in Eastern societies.

- Meeting with someone in public places would be considered something on the borderline, as things might go in the wrong direction starting from this point onwards.

Recommendations

- Be mindful that it is hard to remain pure in the time and society we live in without setting certain rules for ourselves about gender interaction; otherwise, the chances of failure are high.

- When meeting someone of the opposite gender, follow God's fundamental guidance: guard your gaze and dress properly.

- Hang out with people who share our moral values.

- Do not meet a person of the opposite gender in seclusion – even if you like someone, make the meeting a family or friend occasion.

- It is always recommended to involve parents at an early stage if you feel you are in "love" with someone, as this will give you more opportunities to meet in a safer, more protected environment.

- Make interaction purposeful (avoid just passing the time together).

- Avoid indulging in flirtatious conversations – we all know when that moment.

- We should carefully watch our social media interactions and use – meeting someone on a video call is the same as meeting in person (maybe with lesser consequences only at that moment).
- Parents play a critical role in dealing with this issue. They should always think ahead for their growing children and make sure they are ready to support them (emotionally and financially) in case they wish to marry at an early age, without being able to take full financial responsibility.

Q & A and Discussion

Chapter 11

Family related issues

This chapter discusses various topics related to the family institution and the relationship between husband and wife.

Family Related Issues

Introduction

A happy family is the most important building block of a healthy society

ISLAM INSTRUCTS MEN TO BEAT WOMEN

- Interestingly, family matters are among the most discussed topics in the Quran, which provides detailed instructions on them.
- However, some directives in the Quran regarding the rights and duties of husband and wife in a marital relationship have raised concerns that must be understood in their proper contexts.

Family Issues & Misconceptions

- Wife cannot leave the house without the husband's permission
- A wife cannot refuse sex to her husband
- Husband can beat his wife
- Divorce-related issues
- Regarding Halalah
- Polygamy

Family as an institution

- Most problems in a family stem from the fact that husband and wife do not treat it like an institution.
- In the minds of young couples, marriage is usually considered a legal way (Islamically halal) of "spending time together".
- However, in Islam, it is treated like an institution. Like in a business institution, where the welfare of the business is at the heart of everything, in a family institution, the welfare of the children is at the core.
- There are roles, responsibilities, and rights of every member of the family. It runs well when people understand their responsibilities and make all their decisions through mutual consultation in a loving and healthy environment.

1. Wife cannot go out without permission

عَنْ بن عُمَرَ عَنِ النَّبِّي أَنَّ امْرَأَةً أَتَتْهُ فَقَالَتْ مَا حَقُّ الزَّوْجِ عَلَى
امْرَأَتِه فَقَالَ... لاَ تَخْرُجْ مِنْ بَيْتِه إِلاَّ بِإِذْنِه

Ibn Umar reports that the Prophet said that once a lady came to him and asked about the rights of a husband over his wife. He replied: "… She should not leave his house without his permission." (Al Bayhaqi #14490)

- In the institute of marriage, since God has appointed the husband as the head of the household, it makes perfect sense that, to maintain harmony in the household, all activities follow rules and regulations with mutual understanding among its members.
- To understand the matters reported in Ahadith, it is always recommended to look at all the Ahadith on that matter. Looking at Ahadith on family matters, it is clear that this is the Prophet's advice, with the family's welfare and well-being in mind.
- This does not mean that family members cannot disagree with the head of the household; it is his responsibility to run such affairs with mutual consultation and respect, as the head of a state would.
- However, in a state, if differences arise in a family over such matters, the husband will be the final authority.

Key Points
- In Islam, such matters are usually left to mutual understanding among the husband, wife, and other family members, with the culture and norms of society playing a significant role.
- It is quite possible that in a family environment of mutual trust and understanding, a wife need not ask her husband for permission to go out (as we see in our daily lives).
- However, in certain circumstances, if the husband genuinely believes that going out might disrupt the family's well-being, he may exercise his role as head of the household and prevent the wife from leaving the home.
- It should be remembered that such rights do not automatically allow a husband to impose his will on other people without an appropriate and valid reason, and he will be answerable for this act in front of God.

2. Wife cannot refuse sex to the husband

عَنْ أَبِي هُرَيْرَةَ رَضِيَ اللَّهُ عَنْهُ قَالَ قَالَ رَسُولُ اللَّه صَلَّى اللَّهُ عَلَيْهِ
وَسَلَّمَ إِذَا دَعَا الرَّجُلُ امْرَأَتَهُ إِلَى فِرَاشِهِ فَأَبَتْ فَبَاتَ غَضْبَانَ عَلَيْهَا
لَعَنَتْهَا الْمَلَائِكَةُ حَتَّى تُصْبِحَ

Abu Hurairah reported that the Prophet said: "When a husband calls his wife to bed, and she refuses and [as a result] the husband spends the night in anger, then angels curse the wife all night till dawn." (Sahih Bukhari #3237)

- Based on the above hadith, it is generally understood that a wife should not refuse sex to her husband.

- Husband and wife safeguard the chastity of one another by providing a legitimate means to satisfy the sexual needs of one another – this protection of chastity is essential for the preservation of the unit of family.

- If the sexual relationship is limited between husband and wife then it is the responsibility of both (not just wife) to meet each other's needs – for example, in the Quran (2:226-227), God reprimanded the husbands who did "Eila" (An Arab custom in which a husband takes a vow not to have sexual relations with his wife), gave them four months and asked them to either break the vow or divorce their wives instead of leaving them hanging in the marital relationship.

- The above explanation suggests that it is not fitting for a man to deprive his wife of her rights.

- Also, the basis of refusal must be considered before passing any judgment on the wife's action. If either of them is tired, sick, or simply not in the proper mood or frame of mind to have intimacy at that moment, then this cannot be the cause of God's wrath on someone.

Key Points

- Marital life in Islam is based on mercy, love, and tranquility, which can only be maintained through feelings of care and consideration for each other, and not through demanding legal rights from each other.

- It is not a good practice for husbands to quote a hadith from here and there to prove their point or justify their demands without looking at this relationship in the light of the broader framework provided by the religion.

- Just as a housewife must appreciate her husband's efforts to put food on the table, the husband must appreciate and be considerate of his wife's hard work at home and understand how tiring and exhausting it can be.

- Both husband and wife must realize that enjoying intimate time together will only increase their bond of love and is a necessary component of a healthy marriage.

- In the worst-case scenario, if a wife (or husband) refuses for no genuine reason, then this is between her and God and does not give the right to the husband to impose things on her – the best course of action, even in this case, is discussion and dialogue with mutual respect in mind.

أَكْمَلُ الْمُؤْمِنِينَ إِيمَانًا أَحْسَنُهُمْ خُلُقًا وَخِيَارُكُمْ خِيَارُكُمْ لِنِسَائِهِمْ خُلُقًا

"The most complete of believers in faith are those with the best character, and the best of you are the best in behavior to their women." (Sunan Al Tirmidhi #1162)

3. Husband can beat his wife

وَ الَّتِیْ تَخَافُوْنَ نُشُوْزَهُنَّ فَعِظُوْهُنَّ وَ اهْجُرُوْهُنَّ فِی الْمَضَاجِعِ وَ اضْرِبُوْهُنَّ ۚ فَاِنْ اَطَعْنَكُمْ فَلَا تَبْغُوْا عَلَیْهِنَّ سَبِیْلًا

And as for those from whom you fear rebellious behavior, admonish them [first] and [next] refuse to share their beds and [even then if they do not listen] punish them. Then if they obey you, take no further action against them. Indeed, Allah is Exalted and Mighty. (4:34)

- The Quran's giving the right to husbands to strike their wives has been a very controversial topic that many Muslim husbands have also misused in various cultures.

- Before understanding the implications of this verse, it must be refreshed in mind that in the institution of marriage, God has made the husband the head of the household and responsible for the upkeep of the family.

- The following implications of this verse need to be understood in their proper perspective:

  - This measure can only be resorted to when the wife shows a 'rebellious attitude' (*Nushuz*) towards the husband and refuses to accept his authority, and the family is on the brink of breaking apart (*Nushuz* does not mean 'disobedience') - this instruction is very similar to the instruction given to a state to deal with a rebellious citizen.

  - In the process of saving the family from breaking apart (otherwise, the option to divorce is still open), this is the last resort, only after the steps taken in the first two stages have not given any results.

  - From the study of various narratives of the Prophet, it is clear that the punishment or admonishment is more of the nature of reprimand, not of violence or torture, to produce positive results, not to vent one's rage, and must not result in any type of physical injury.

  - Exercising one's right is a choice that must be made with prudence, keeping the norms of the society and the circumstances one lives in – if any reprimand is counter-productive, one should not use it at all.

فَضَرَبَ صَلَّى اللّٰهُ عَلَيْهِ وَسَلَّمَ بِيَدِهِ عَلَى مَنْكِبِي ثُمَّ قَالَ

The Prophet (SAW) struck my chest with his hand, and said... (Sahih Muslim #1825)

- Most early commentators of the Quran understood the word 'strike' as a symbolic gesture of displeasure that should not cause pain. For example, in this hadith, the word 'daraba' is used.

Key Points

وَ جَعَلَ بَيْنَكُم مَّوَدَّةً وَّ رَحْمَةً

And He has placed between husband and wife, love and mercy. (30:21)

- Topics like this are controversial because people view these directives through a modern-day lens, even though societal norms have changed.
- Most men tend to use physical force when they want to rebuke their wives. The Quran, through this directive, has restricted reproach to extreme situations (challenging the authority of the husband) and also as the final resort (not the first) – the hope is to achieve some positive results; otherwise, it must be avoided.
- If the husband adopts the methodology suggested by the Quran with sincerity, then it is highly likely that the matter will be resolved by taking the first two steps.
- If the husband misuses his authority in any way, he would not only be held responsible in the court of law but also before the Almighty on the Day of Judgment.
- In today's society, if the state recognizes that husbands are misusing this directive, it can enact laws to prohibit such misuse and require husbands to bring the matter to court.

4. Divorce related Issues

1 What is the correct method for divorce?

2 Do women have the right to divorce?

3 Should the wife pay the money to seek a divorce?

4 How to deal with a divorce in which the method was violated?

5 Who should have the custody of the child after divorce?

4.1 The Correct Method of Divorce

اَلطَّلَاقُ مَرَّتْنِ فَاِمْسَاكٌ بِمَعْرُوْفٍ اَوْ تَسْرِيْحٌ بِاِحْسَانٍ

The divorce can be pronounced twice (in one relationship), then, either holding with kindness or leaving with grace. (2:231)

Initiation

1. Divorce should be initiated (uttering words like "I divorce you" one time or in writing) only after the woman has completed her monthly menstrual cycle, in the period of cleanliness in which the husband did not have any sexual relations with her.
2. The number of days starting from the initiation of the divorce until the end of the waiting period must be carefully counted.
3. During this time, the woman would stay in her husband's house, and the husband is responsible for providing for her (she may stay elsewhere if they both agree).

Separation

1. Once the waiting period expires and the husband decides not to take back his decision, the relationship of wedlock between husband and wife ceases at that moment.

2. If the husband has initiated the divorce, he should not take back any gifts of wealth, jewelry, property, clothing, or other items given to the wife. Two exceptions: a) if the wife asked for the divorce and the husband hesitates to divorce due to financial loss, and both agreed that the wife should return something, and b) the wife has committed adultery.

3. The husband is not responsible for giving the dower at the time of divorce if no physical relationship was established with the wife. However, if the dower has already been agreed upon, then he should pay half of the agreed-upon amount (2:236-237). God has advised the husband to be generous, to relinquish his rights, and to give more than is due as a sign of piety and manhood.

4. At the time of separation, God asked the husband to provide financial support to the departing wife so she could sustain herself before she remarried (2:241, 2:236).

5. This completes one divorce between the husband and the wife.

6. Both can remarry each other or with anyone they want.

7. If both decide to remarry, all conditions and procedures for a new marriage will be applied.

Revocation

1. If the husband decides to revoke his decision of divorce before the waiting period ends, then, according to the Quran, he has exercised one of his rights to divorce with the liberty to revoke it. A husband can only exercise this right twice in one marriage in which he has permission to withdraw it. If he divorces for the third time, he cannot revoke it.

2. God has cautioned the husband that if he decides to revoke his decision, then it should not be to hurt or harass her – God calls this act equal to making a mockery of God's commandments, which is a severe crime in the sight of God.

3. If the husband has already exercised his right to divorce twice, then the third time, the only option is permanent separation until the condition to remarry is met.

4. The only way they can remarry is if the wife gets divorced from another man or her new husband dies; however, this CAN NOT be planned; this is a great sin in Islam.

A Short Summary of the Divorce Process

1. This is the only method of divorce prescribed in Shariah.

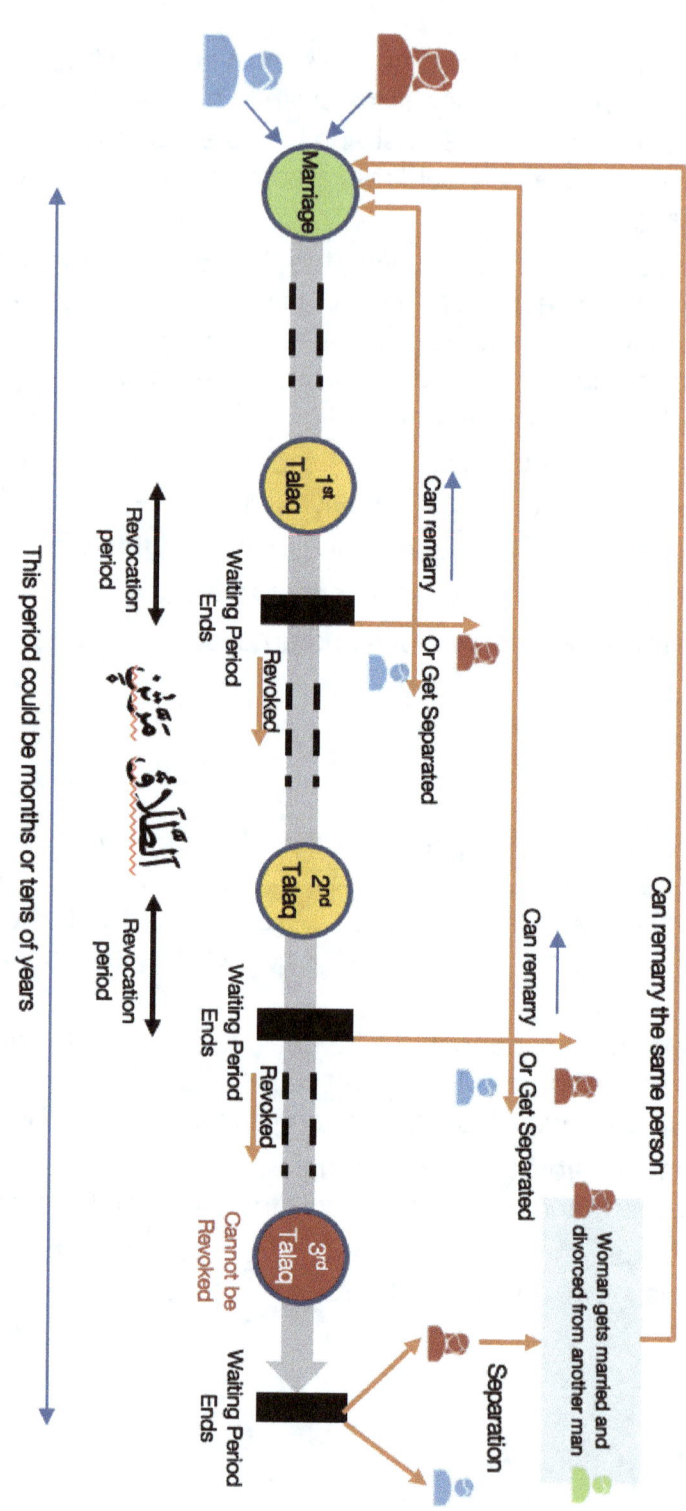

4.2 Do women have the right to divorce?

Then, if you also feel that they will not be able to remain within the bounds set by Allah, there shall be no offense for either of them [regarding the gifts given by the husband] if the wife seeks divorce [by returning them to him] in ransom. (2:229)

- The husband has been made head of the household and given the responsibility for earning and providing for the family.
- Given the nature of his responsibilities and status, the Quran grants the husband the authority to initiate divorce.
- Entrusting two people with different responsibilities but granting them equal rights to establish or dismantle an organization cannot keep that institution functioning – a person with more responsibilities should have greater rights.
- When a woman seeks a separation from her husband, she must ask her husband to grant her a divorce. God made it mandatory for the husband to comply with the demand after a reconciliation process, as recommended by the Quran.
- If the husband does not comply with the wife's demand, the wife can seek assistance from his family, his tribe, or the court of law.

The wife of Thabit ibn Qais once came to the Prophet and said: "O Messenger of Allah! I do not have any complaints regarding his character and person; however, I fear losing my faith." When the Prophet heard this complaint, he said: "Would you return his orchard?" She showed her consent. At this, the Prophet directed Thabit to accept the orchard and separate her by pronouncing one divorce sentence. (Sahih Al-Bukhari 5273, 5277)

> The simple rule is: a man divorces his wife, while a woman demands a divorce from her husband; if there is no way to reconcile, he should initiate the divorce.

4.3 Should the wife pay money to seek a divorce?

اَلطَّلَاقُ مَرَّتٰنِ ۖ فَاِمْسَاكٌ بِمَعْرُوْفٍ اَوْ تَسْرِيْحٌ بِاِحْسَانٍ ۗ وَ لَا يَحِلُّ لَكُمْ اَنْ تَأْخُذُوْا مِمَّآ اٰتَيْتُمُوْهُنَّ شَيْئًا اِلَّآ اَنْ يَّخَافَآ اَلَّا يُقِيْمَا حُدُوْدَ اللّٰهِ ۖ فَاِنْ خِفْتُمْ اَلَّا يُقِيْمَا حُدُوْدَ اللّٰهِ ۙ فَلَا جُنَاحَ عَلَيْهِمَا فِيْمَا افْتَدَتْ بِهٖ ۗ تِلْكَ حُدُوْدُ اللّٰهِ فَلَا تَعْتَدُوْهَا ۚ وَ مَنْ يَّتَعَدَّ حُدُوْدَ اللّٰهِ فَاُولٰٓئِكَ هُمُ الظّٰلِمُوْنَ

And it is unlawful for you [on this occasion] to take back from them anything you have given them unless both husband and wife fear that they may not be able to keep within the bounds set by Allah. Then, if you also feel that they will not be able to remain within the bounds set by Allah, there shall be no offense for either of them [regarding the gifts given by the husband] if the wife seeks divorce [by returning them to him] in ransom. These are the bounds set by Allah, so do not transgress them. And [you should know that] those who violate the bounds of Allah are wrongdoers. (2:229)

- According to the Quran, at the time of separation, it is not at all permissible for the husband to demand anything from his wife on this occasion except:
  - The husband has gifted a lot of wealth and property to his wife, or may have gifted her something essential for his livelihood (or significant to him), and is afraid that divorcing her would severely impact him financially – the wife can forego something to get the divorce in return.
  - The wife is guilty of open sexual misconduct. (Surah Nisa 19-21)

4.4 Divorce, which violates the procedure

- In our daily lives, as in any other matter, people make mistakes due to ignorance and do not follow the divorce procedure prescribed by Shariah.
- Contrary to the intention of Shariah, most of the time, the divorce is declared when the husband is extremely emotionally charged and wants to end the marital relationship immediately.
- When a mistake is made in declaring the divorce, it comes in the category of "breach of the law," and in the absence of any rulings given in Shariah to handle the breach, it is up to the state legislation or the judge to deal with such cases, assuming that common sense and the norms of the society prevail.

Major types of deviation or breach

1. A husband divorces his wife during her menstrual period or divorces her after he has had a physical relationship with her during her period of purity.
2. A husband divorces his wife by pronouncing the divorce sentence thrice with no regard to the fact that he has multiple chances to divorce in this marriage (as per the injunctions of the Quran).

Dealing with two types of deviations

A: Wrong time for divorce

- When Abdullah ibn Umar divorced his wife during her menstrual cycle, the Prophet was upset and remarked:

مرة فَلْيُرَاجِعْهَا ثُمَّ لِيُمْسِكْهَا حتى تَطْهُرَ ثُمَّ تَحِيضَ ثُمَّ تَطْهُرُ ثُمَّ إن شَاءَ أَمْسَكَ بَعْدُ وَإِنْ شَاءَ طَلَّقَ قبل أَنْ يَمَسَّ فَتِلْكَ الْعِدَّةُ التي أَمَرَ الله أَنْ تُطَلَّقَ لها النِّسَاءُ

Ask him to take her back and keep her in wedlock until she is through with her menstrual cycle, and then once again passes through this cycle and is through with it. After this, he can either detain her [in wedlock] or divorce her before having sexual intercourse with her. Because it is the beginning of the waiting period, keeping regard of which the Almighty has directed [believers] to divorce their wives. (Sahih Al-Bukhari #4953).

- The Islamic state or the judge can ask the husband to revoke his decision and carry it out again properly at the proper time.
- Some other decisions can be made depending on the situation, but the most appropriate ruling has already been given by the Prophet in his time, because if all aspects are not considered and divorce is declared, the case may become complicated if the wife becomes pregnant after the divorce.

B: Triple divorce at once

- The husband can be called to court and asked about the true intention behind this declaration.
- He might testify that it was all said and done in anger, that he only intended to divorce once, or that he had no intention of divorcing; then the court/state can reunite the husband and wife.
- Or he might testify and say that he has consciously uttered these words three times because he had the intention to use all the chances of divorce at once, and in that case, the court/judge may decide to declare this divorce valid and separate them (such an event occurred in the lifetime of the Prophet, recorded in Sunan Abu Daud #2206).
- The state, after observing that people are negligent about following the proper method of divorce and have adopted a carefree attitude towards it, might legislate that if someone comes with a triple divorce situation, they will not be given any chance to take it back, and the divorce will be pronounced.

- The state, also, after observing that people are ignorant of the correct method, may legislate that regardless of the number of times the words are uttered, it will always be counted as one.
- Umar bin Khattab, the second Caliph, did the same. When the cases of divorce came to him, and he noticed that people had started misusing their right to three divorces, he made a law that, from now on, husbands' excuses will not be accepted, and their three divorces will be considered as if they have used their right of three divorces at once, and they cannot marry their wives anymore.
- It was a kind of punishment for the husbands from the state due to their negligent behavior and attitude of playing with the religion of God.

4.5 Custody of the children

- In case of young children or the birth of a newborn at the time of divorce, if the mother is willing to suckle the children, then the husband shall pay her for this service, and this remuneration shall be ascertained through mutual consultation and in a befitting manner (he will pay her some money as living expenses until she suckles the child).
- Shariah is quiet about the custody of the children, as varying circumstances may demand varying rulings depending on the welfare of the children and also the situation of the parents.
- For teenagers, the judge may ask the children about their preferred person to stay with after the separation, or may decide based on the children's welfare.
- When it comes to the custody of minors who cannot decide on their own, it is left up to the judge to rule according to the situation and circumstances, keeping the welfare of the children in mind.

5. Halalah

The concept of Halalah is alien to *Shariah* and is one of the ugliest and most shameful issues of Islamic jurisprudence.

Ahmed marries Maryam and after the third divorce they got separated

Abdullah marries Maryam and divorces her for the first time, and they get separated

Ahmed remarries Maryam and starts a new marital life with her

Maryam Ahmed

Maryam Abdullah

Maryam Ahmed

Time

Legal requirement **for Ahmed to remarry Maryam**

- Islam did <u>not</u> define the process of *Halalah*. What the Quran describes is the legal condition for remarriage and a situation that might occur in their lifetime. **THIS IS NOT A PROCEDURE.**
- To meet the legal requirement for Ahmed to marry Maryam again, people have introduced trickery and 'planned marriages', a procedure in which people are available to play the role of Abdullah.
- On top of that, Islamic jurists have added a condition that Abdullah must have consummated the marriage before divorcing Maryam.
- This middle step, in which Abdullah marries Maryam and then divorces her after consummating the marriage so she becomes legal again for Ahmed, is called *Halalah*.
- These tricks amount to playing with Islamic law and its spirit, and are completely prohibited.
- The condition of consummation of the marriage has been added due to a misunderstanding of a subtle comment made by the Prophet in a case reported in the books of Ahadith.
- A case was presented to the Prophet, and it was clear that the woman had married the other man to meet the legal requirement to remarry her previous husband. She immediately demanded a divorce from the man right after the marriage on false grounds that her husband was sexually impotent.
- When the Prophet realized her scheme, he reprimanded her and told her she could only become permissible for the first husband after "tasting" her second husband – the Prophet meant to discourage the concept and wanted to teach her a lesson this way, and this cannot be taken as a condition added by the Prophet.

Ikramah narrates that Rifaah divorced his wife. After that, she married Abd al-Rahman al Quraz. Ayesha says that she came to her wearing a green cloak and complained of her husband and showed Ayesha her bruises – women do help one another – so when the Prophet came by, Ayesha said: "I have only seen Muslim women being treated in such a way. Her skin is greener than her cloak." Ikramah says that when her husband learned she had complained to the Prophet, he also came to the Prophet with his two sons from his other wife. Upon seeing her husband, she got hold of the end of her cloak, letting it hang from her hand, and remarked: My only complaint is that whatever he has is no more than his [soft cloth]. At this, Abd al Rahman said: "O Prophet of Allah! She has told a lie. I am very strong and can [sexually] satisfy her; the truth of the matter is that she is disobedient and wants to return to Rifaah." When the Prophet heard this, he said, "If this is the case, then you shall not be permissible for Rifaah unless Abd al Rahman tastes you." Then, upon seeing the sons of Abd al Rahman, the Prophet remarked, "Are these your sons?" When he replied in the affirmative, the Prophet said: "Do you tell such lies [O Abd al Rahman's wife]. By God! These [young boys] resemble 'Abd al Rahman more than a crow resembles another crow."

6. Polygamy

وَ اِنْ خِفْتُمْ اَلَّا تُقْسِطُوْا فِى الْيَتٰمٰى فَانْكِحُوْا مَا طَابَ لَكُمْ مِّنَ النِّسَاءِ مَثْنٰى وَ ثُلٰثَ وَ رُبٰعَ ۚ فَاِنْ خِفْتُمْ اَلَّا تَعْدِلُوْا
فَوَاحِدَةً اَوْ مَا مَلَكَتْ اَيْمَانُكُمْ ۗ ذٰلِكَ اَدْنٰى اَلَّا تَعُوْلُوْا وَ اٰتُوا النِّسَاءَ صَدُقٰتِهِنَّ نِحْلَةً ۚ فَاِنْ طِبْنَ لَكُمْ عَنْ شَىْءٍ مِّنْهُ
نَفْسًا فَكُلُوْهُ هَنِيْئًا مَّرِيْئًا

And if you fear that you shall not be able to deal justly with the orphans, marry [their mothers] who are lawful to you, two two, three three, four four; but if you fear that you shall not be able to deal justly [with them], then only one, or those which your right hands possess. That will be more suitable to prevent you from doing injustice. And give these women their dowers also the way dowers are given; but if they, of their own good pleasure, remit any part of it to you, take it and consume it gladly. (4:3-4)

- It is quite misleading to say that "Islam allowed four marriages".
- Islam or any other religion did not start the practice of polygamy; social, psychological, political, and cultural needs gave rise to the need for polygamy, and such needs existed in various societies.
- The verses related to polygamy came in the context of guardianship of the orphans after the Battle of Uhud. God appealed to the guardians, saying that if they cannot deal justly with the orphans while discharging their responsibilities, then they should marry their mothers and bring them into their family circle.
- The context suggests that the verses were not explicitly revealed for the allowance of polygamy, as some people suggest – the verses imply that, since men were already marrying more than one woman in that society, why not the guardians do the same for the welfare of the children?
- However, the Shariah put two conditions on it: one cannot marry more than 4 women, and they should be dealt with justice as much as possible.
- So the correct conclusion should be that Islam restricted the number of wives to four at a time.
- Prophet Muhammad was given an exception to this rule due to his role as a Messenger in the latter part of his life. Most of his marriages, except 3 were direct results of God's command to him as His Messenger. His marriage to Zaynab was even discussed in Surah Ahzab.
- It is interesting to note that, despite the culture of marrying multiple women, he did not marry any other woman during his marriage to Khadija (which lasted almost 25 years).

Q & A and Discussion

Chapter 12

Women-related issues

This chapter discusses various topics related to women in Islam. Most people consider Islam a patriarchal religion with no regard for women.

Women Related Issues

Introduction

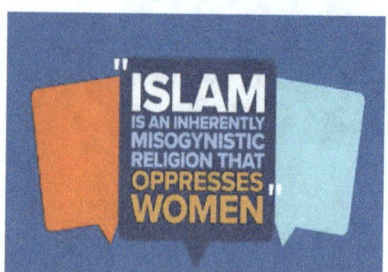

- The issues related to women in Islam are among the most misunderstood and misinterpreted subjects throughout history.
- These misunderstandings are primarily the product of various patriarchal cultures where Islam was the dominant religion of the population and had nothing to do with the faith of Islam itself.
- This challenge of mixing religion with local culture (especially tribal culture) was not clearly addressed by scholars of Islam because some aspects of religion helped mold the entire civilization, and many such women-related issues were usually acceptable (or overlooked) in society. Now that we are living in the 21st century, the century of freedom, people have begun to take notice of the issues that various scholars of Islam are trying to address.
- One of the aftermaths of this negligence is that those scholars of Islam, who try to address these misunderstandings, face backlash from their own communities due to "modernizing Islam".

Women Issues

- The following issues related to women will be discussed in this chapter:

  1. Women are less intelligent than men.
  2. Women cannot travel without a male relative.
  3. Women will outnumber men in Hell.
  4. Women are inferior to men.

1. Women are less intelligent than men

عَنْ أَبِي سَعِيد الْخُدْرِيّ قَالَ خَرَجَ رَسُولُ اللَّه صَلَّى اللَّهُ عَلَيْه
وَسَلَّمَ فِي أَضْحَى أَوْ فِطْرٍ إِلَى الْمُصَلَّى فَمَرَّ عَلَى النِّسَاء فَقَالَ... مَا
رَأَيْتُ مِنْ نَاقِصَاتِ عَقْلٍ وَدِينٍ أَذْهَبَ لِلُبِّ الرَّجُلِ الْحَازِمِ مِنْ
إِحْدَاكُنَّ قُلْنَ وَمَا نُقْصَانُ دِينِنَا وَعَقْلِنَا يَا رَسُولَ اللَّه قَالَ أَلَيْسَ
شَهَادَةُ الْمَرْأَة مِثْلَ نِصْفِ شَهَادَة الرَّجُلِ قُلْنَ بَلَى قَالَ فَذَلِكَ مِنْ
نُقْصَانِ عَقْلِهَا أَلَيْسَ إِذَا حَاضَتْ لَمْ تُصَلِّ وَلَمْ تَصُمْ قُلْنَ بَلَى قَالَ
فَذَلِكَ مِنْ نُقْصَانِ دِينِهَا

Abu Said al Khudri narrated: "Once the Prophet set off for the prayer place on Eid al Fitr or Eid al Adha. He passed by a group of women and said: '… and I have seen no one more than you rob even a resolute man of his senses despite being *naqisat e aql wa din*.' They said: 'O Allah's Messenger! What is this naqs in our religious and worldly affairs?' He said: 'Is not the evidence of a woman equal to half of a man?' They said: 'Yes.' He said: 'This is the naqs in their worldly affairs.' He said: 'Is it not a fact that when they enter the period of menses, they neither pray nor fast.' They said: 'Yes.' Whereupon he said: 'This is the naqs in their religious affairs.'" (Sahih Al Bukhari #298)

- The hadith above is often quoted to support the argument that women are less intelligent.
- The confusion arose from the incorrect translation of the word naqs, which is generally understood in Urdu as "defective."
- In Arabic, the verb Naqasa means "to reduce" or "reduction in something."
- This hadith refers to the fact that women are given a reduction in both worldly and religious affairs:
  - In Surah Baqarah verse 282, the Quran urges men to testify on legal documents so that women are not burdened with appearing in courts, as they usually feel uncomfortable with such activities in most societies. The Quran even instructs to take two women if men are not available, so that they can support each other.
  - In religious affairs, women are not required to pray or fast during their menstrual cycles.
  - Similarly, they are not asked to join the fighting if Muslims were asked to fight a war for some reason.

Key Points

- The meaning of a word does not always remain the same in two different languages, even if it originated from one of them. That's precisely what happened with the word "Naqs". Another example is "Ghaleez," which means "firm" in Arabic but "dirty" in Urdu.

- The hadith refers not only to *Naqisat al Aql* (worldly affairs) but also to Naqisat e Din, which, if understood in the same way people do, would imply that their religion has a defect that is unfair and makes no sense.

- The Quran's suggestion to take two women as witnesses for legal documents, primarily related to financial matters, is intended to protect the lender. This is not an instruction. In those times, women's main focus was generally on their households rather than on financial matters.

- Regarding judicial/civil proceedings, there is no restriction on who may serve as a witness, as this depends on the circumstances.

2. Women cannot travel alone

لَا يُحِلُّ لِامْرَأَةٍ تُؤْمِنُ بِاللهِ وَالْيَوْمِ الآخِرِ تُسَافِرُ مَسِيرَةَ يَوْمٍ وَلَيْلَةٍ إِلاَّ
مَعَ ذِي مَحْرَمٍ عَلَيْهَا

"It is not permissible for a woman who believes in Allah and the Last Day to travel a distance for one day and one night without a mahram with her. (Sahih Muslim #1339)

نُهِيَ أَنْ تُسَافِرَ الْمَرْأَةَ مَسِيرَةَ يَوْمَيْنِ إِلَّا وَمَعَهَا زَوْجَهَا أَوْ ذُوْ مَحْرَمٍ

A woman was stopped from travelling a distance for two days except with her husband or mahram with her." (Sahih Muslim #827)

- Most scholars use the Ahadith above to form an opinion that Muslim women cannot travel alone, which has been extended by some to the idea that they should not leave the house without a mahram.

- This has been adopted in many state laws; for example, women were not allowed to undertake the Hajj journey alone.

- All such directives given by the Prophet are for the well-being of the Muslims and must be understood in the conditions and environment of those times.

- Such directives may no longer apply when the situation or circumstances change.

- In those times, traveling alone was not considered safe for women. The Prophet gave these instructions to protect women from the dangers of long journeys and any scandalous allegation in the strife-ridden society of Arabia.
- These days, travel conditions are very different, and every woman traveler must decide for herself whether the journey is safe enough to travel alone.
- It is important to note that the situation changed right after the time of the Prophet – he predicted in a hadith that a woman from Sana'a would travel to Makkah alone and would have no fear but of Allah. Adi ibn Hatim, who reported this hadith, said that he witnessed that situation.

3. Women will outnumber men in Hell

عَنْ أَبِي سَعِيدٍ الْخُدْرِيِّ قَالَ خَرَجَ رَسُولُ اللَّهِ صَلَّى اللَّهُ عَلَيْهِ وَسَلَّمَ
فِي أَضْحَى أَوْ فِطْرٍ إِلَى الْمُصَلَّى فَمَرَّ عَلَى النِّسَاءِ فَقَالَ يَا مَعْشَرَ
النِّسَاءِ تَصَدَّقْنَ فَإِنِّي أُرِيتُكُنَّ أَكْثَرَ أَهْلِ النَّارِ فَقُلْنَ وَبِمَ يَا رَسُولَ اللَّهِ
قَالَ تُكْثِرْنَ اللَّعْنَ وَتَكْفُرْنَ الْعَشِيرَ

Abu Said al-Khudri reported: "Allah's Messenger went out to the place of prayer on the day of Eid al-Adha or Fitr. So, he passed by some women and said to them: 'O Women, give charity for I have been shown the majority amongst you as the inmates of Hell.' They said: 'Allah's Messenger, wherefore?' He said: 'It is because you curse one another very much and show ungratefulness to your husbands.'" (Sahih Al-Bukhari #298)

- Prophets are shown, such as Roya, or dreams, a source of revelation, for either giving news about the future or educating the believers – these dreams are symbolic and require interpretation.
- Symbolic representation is a powerful form of expression and conveys the message most comprehensively – one can see this in poetry.
- The idea is to look beyond the apparent, reflect, discover, and infer from what has been shown – a good example is the dreams of Prophet Yusuf.
- The showing of a greater number of women in Hell must be related to the deeds that the Prophet had described later in the hadith. The idea is to warn women that certain deeds will cause more women to fail in the Hereafter than men, and women must be aware of them and avoid them.

4. Women are inferior to men

وَ لِلرِّجَالِ عَلَيْهِنَّ دَرَجَةٌ

And the husbands hold a degree of superiority over them. (2:228)

اَلرِّجَالُ قَوَّمُوْنَ عَلَى النِّسَآءِ بِمَا فَضَّلَ اللهُ بَعْضَهُمْ عَلَى بَعْضٍ وَّ بِمَآ اَنْفَقُوْا مِنْ اَمْوَالِهِمْ

Men are the guardians of women, because God has given one more preference over the other, and because they support them. (4:34)

عن أبي هُرَيْرَةَ رضي الله عنه قال قال رسول الله صلى الله عليه
وسلم اسْتَوْصُوا بالنِّسَاء فإن الْمَرْأَةَ خُلِقَتْ من ضِلَعٍ وَإِنَّ أَعْوَجَ
شَيْءٍ في الضِّلَعِ أَعْلَاهُ فإِنْ ذَهَبْتَ تُقِيمُهُ كَسَرْتَهُ وَإِنْ تَرَكْتَهُ لم يَزَلْ
أَعْوَجَ فَاسْتَوْصُوا بالنِّسَاء

Abu Hurairah reports that Allah's Prophet said: "Treat women nicely, for a woman is created from a rib, and the most curved portion of the rib is its upper portion; so, if you should try to straighten it, it will break, but if you leave it as it is, it will remain crooked. So, treat women nicely." (Sahih al Bukhari #3153)

- On the basis of the above verses and hadith, it is argued by some people that men are superior to women.
- It needs to be appreciated that the verses of Surah Baqarah and Surah Nisaa relate to the responsibilities of **husband and wife** in a family, **not to men and women** in general.
- In the institution of family, God has entrusted men with the responsibility of being the head of the household, and he is considered 'superior' in that aspect.
- Men are granted this status for two reasons:
  - They are physically and temperamentally stronger and better able to take care of the entire family.
  - They are responsible for all financial matters and the upkeep of the family, including the children.
- There are certain spheres of life in which wives, by nature, are superior to husbands and are much more suitable to do certain tasks. For example, they are good at multitasking and management, more disciplined, patient, and forbearing, all of which are good traits in a family.

- The differences in the rights and responsibilities are in the context of relationships. For e.g., a mother, being a woman, has more rights over their children and deserves more respect and companionship from their children than their father (as mentioned in one of the Ahadith).

Relationships are not equal

Men and Women are created equal

يَٰٓأَيُّهَا ٱلنَّاسُ ٱتَّقُوا۟ رَبَّكُمُ ٱلَّذِى خَلَقَكُم مِّن نَّفْسٍ وَٰحِدَةٍ وَّ خَلَقَ مِنْهَا زَوْجَهَا وَ بَثَّ مِنْهُمَا رِجَالًا كَثِيرًا وَّ نِسَآءً ۚ وَ اتَّقُوا۟ ٱللَّهَ ٱلَّذِى تَسَآءَلُونَ بِهِ وَ ٱلْأَرْحَامَ ۚ إِنَّ ٱللَّهَ كَانَ عَلَيْكُمْ رَقِيبًا

Mankind! Fear your Lord, Who created you from a single person and created, of like species, his mate, and from these two scattered countless men and women [in this world], and fear Allah through whom you seek mutual help and fear breaking blood relationships. Indeed, God is watching over you. (4:1)

- Verse 4:1 of the Quran provides a completely different account from what is commonly understood from the hadith (that Eve was created from Adam's rib). According to the Quran, men and women, as human beings, are created from a single soul/entity, and all humanity is created from them.
- Some have misinterpreted the verse as "created you from a single person (Adam), and then He created from him, his wife (Eve)".
- The words خَلَقَ مِنْهَا زَوْجَهَا imply that his wife was also created from the same species or entity as Adam. This point is emphasized in another verse:

وَ ٱللَّهُ جَعَلَ لَكُم مِّنْ أَنفُسِكُمْ أَزْوَٰجًا

And it is God who has made from your species/entity you mates (16:72)

- 'From you' here cannot mean 'from your physical body' but only 'from the same species as yours.'

Key Points

- In the aforementioned hadith, the statement, "a woman is created from a rib," does not necessarily refer to the physical material of creation but can also refer to the nature or essence of something. For e.g., the Quran says:

Man has been created from (the extract/nature of) haste (21:37)

- Looking at all the textual variants of this hadith, it is clear that the Prophet was alluding to the 'nature of the women' when comparing it to a rib, meaning that the nature of the women is very delicate and tender, as well as a bit firm/fixed. The Prophet advised men that when dealing with women, they should not force anything on them but try to persuade and convince them. Because if they try to force anything on them, it will make matters more complex (that's what he means by 'it will break').

إِنَّ الْمُسْلِمِيْنَ وَ الْمُسْلِمٰتِ وَ الْمُؤْمِنِيْنَ وَ الْمُؤْمِنٰتِ وَ الْقٰنِتِيْنَ وَ الْقٰنِتٰتِ وَ الصّٰدِقِيْنَ وَ الصّٰدِقٰتِ وَ الصّٰبِرِيْنَ وَ الصّٰبِرٰتِ وَ الْخٰشِعِيْنَ وَ الْخٰشِعٰتِ وَ الْمُتَصَدِّقِيْنَ وَ الْمُتَصَدِّقٰتِ وَ الصَّآئِمِيْنَ وَ الصّٰئِمٰتِ وَ الْحٰفِظِيْنَ فُرُوْجَهُمْ وَ الْحٰفِظٰتِ وَ الذّٰكِرِيْنَ اللهَ كَثِيْرًا وَّ الذّٰكِرٰتِ ۙ اَعَدَّ اللهُ لَهُمْ مَّغْفِرَةً وَّ اَجْرًا عَظِيْمًا

Surely the men who submit and the women who submit, and the believing men and the believing women, and the obeying men and the obeying women, and the truthful men and the truthful women, and the patient men and the patient women and the humble men and the humble women, and the almsgiving men and the almsgiving women, and the fasting men and the fasting women, and the men who guard their private parts and the women who guard, and the men who remember Allah much and the women who remember. Allah has prepared for them (both) forgiveness and a mighty reward. (33:35)

Q & A and Discussion

Chapter 13

Slavery and Sex with Slave Women

This chapter discusses another issue that has been somehow labelled with Islam, although at the time of Prophet Muhammad, these issues existed in the society and around him, and that is slavery.

The practice of Slavery

Introduction

Is there slavery in Islam?

Wrong question

Slavery's Roots: War and Economic Domination

- **6800 B.C.** The world's first city-state emerges in Mesopotamia. Land ownership and the early stages of technology bring war—in which enemies are captured and forced to work: slavery.
- **2575 B.C.** Temple art celebrates the capture of slaves in battle. Egyptians capture slaves by sending special expeditions up the Nile River.
- **550 B.C.** The city-state of Athens uses as many as 30,000 slaves in its silver mines.
- **120 A.D.** Roman military campaigns capture slaves by the thousands. Some estimate the population of Rome is more than half slave.
- **500** Anglo-Saxons enslave the native Britons after invading England.
- **1000** Slavery is a normal practice in England's rural, agricultural economy, as destitute workers place themselves and their families in a form of debt bondage to landowners.
- **1380** In the aftermath of the Black Plague, Europe's slave trade thrives in response to a labor shortage. Slaves pour in from all over the continent, the Middle East, and North Africa.
- **1444** Portuguese traders bring the first large cargo of slaves from West Africa to Europe by sea—establishing the Atlantic slave trade.
- **1526** Spanish explorers bring the first African slaves to settlements in what would become the United States. These first African-Americans stage the first known slave revolt in the Americas.
- **1550** Slaves are depicted as objects of conspicuous consumption in much Renaissance art.
- **1641** Massachusetts becomes the first British colony to legalize slavery.

Source: freetheslaves.net

- According to some historians, the history of slavery as an institution is more than 8000 years old and has existed in every culture and society of the world.
- The source of slavery was warfare, in which the prisoners of war were turned into slaves and sold in the marketplaces, which then contributed to the economic engine of the society.
- At the time of Prophet Muhammad, the Arab tribes used to fight long wars, and the victor used to take people into slavery as a symbol of dominance over the tribe that they defeated.
- There is a misconception about Islam that it gives sanction to slavery and permits its followers to enslave prisoners of war.
- The confusion arose from the fact that Islam did not abolish the institution of slavery and adopted a gradual process to abolish it over a period of time (at least that was the intent).
- The other factor that contributed to this perception was the practice of the later Muslim rulers who came after the Rightly-Guided Caliphs and displayed a nonchalant behavior towards slavery, and slavery remained alive in the Muslim world.

Why did Islam not abolish slavery?

- Slavery was an institution and the backbone of the economic engine of the Arab society at the time of Prophet Muhammad.

- Thousands of slaves used to earn a living for their masters and, as a result, were cared for by the masters – they used to take trade caravans to distant places, raise livestock and do farming, and perform skilled labor like making swords and arrows.

- It is God's practice that one can learn from the Quran that if a bad social practice becomes part of the fabric of society and social conditions do not allow abolishing it immediately, then He recommends a gradual path with clear steps towards its eradication - that's exactly the approach that Islam took towards eradicating slavery.

- There were scores of slaves that were part of every household, coming from two sources: prisoners of war distributed as slaves and slaves bought in the marketplaces.

- An immediate order of prohibition or abolishment would have created an immense economic and social mess in that society, with thousands of young and old slaves on the street with no means to earn, and slave girls would be forced to sell their bodies to earn money.

- The initial followers of Islam were very loyal to the Prophet and Islam, and a single instruction of prohibition would be enough for them to emancipate all the slaves.

- The situation can be understood by looking at the current economic situation – abolishing interest suddenly in an Islamic society would result in the collapse of the entire economy.

Islam's approach towards abolishment

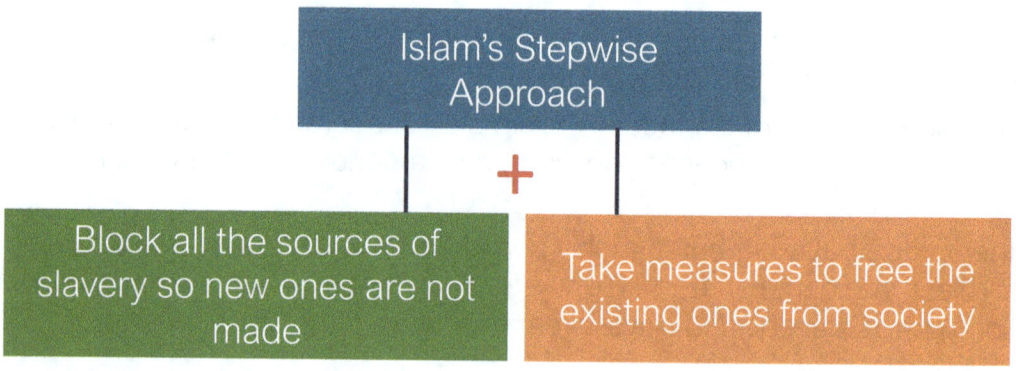

Islam's approach towards abolishment

فَإِذَا لَقِيتُمُ الَّذِينَ كَفَرُوا فَضَرْبَ الرِّقَابِ ۖ حَتَّىٰ إِذَا أَثْخَنتُمُوهُمْ فَشُدُّوا الْوَثَاقَ ۚ فَإِمَّا مَنًّا بَعْدُ
وَ إِمَّا فِدَآءً حَتَّىٰ تَضَعَ الْحَرْبُ أَوْزَارَبَا

So, when you encounter the disbelievers in a battle, smite at their necks until you overpower them, then take them as captives when they are defeated. <u>Then you may set them free as a favor to them, or in exchange for a ransom,</u> when the battle lays its arms. (Surah Muhammad: 4)

Block the source

- Since wars were the main source of slavery, where captives from the other side were made slaves and then sold in the market, Islam banned the idea of taking captives in wars permanently. In Surah Muhammad, which was revealed at the time of the Battle of Badr, God told Muslims to either set the captives free as a favor or take ransom in exchange.
- Reading the history of the Battle of Badr, people can relate that this is exactly what happened after the battle. Prophet Muhammad took one of the above approaches to release all of the prisoners of war.

Measures to free existing ones gradually

- In the early Makkan period, the Quran declared slave emancipation a great act of piety.
- The Prophet directed the Muslims to raise the standard of living of the slaves and treat them equally in their homes.
- It was set as an atonement for many sins by God.
- All slaves who could support themselves in society were directed to marry one another.
- A permanent head in the public treasury was fixed to set free slaves.
- Prostitution, largely carried out through slave women, was outlawed.
- People were encouraged to call them boys or girls instead of slaves (Abd).
- Finally, the law of Mukatibat was introduced, allowing slaves to enter into a contract with their masters to gain their freedom if they paid the agreed amount within the specified time.

In the lifetime of the Prophet

- About 70 prisoners of the Battle of Badr were either freed for ransom or taught how to write by the children of Ansar.

- After the battle of Mustaliq, the Prophet brought some POWs back to Medinah, having freed many in the battle, either as a favor or for ransom. He temporarily gave them into the custody of the companions. Sayyidah Jaweriah was among them. When her father came to ransom her against a few camels, the Prophet inquired about the two well-bred camels that he had left behind. The father was amazed and realized that Prophet Muhammad was a true Prophet; otherwise, he had no way to know about those two camels. The Prophet extended a marriage proposal to Jaweriah, and she and her father accepted it. As a result, the companions freed the captives, as they had become the Prophet's in-laws.

- In the Battle of Hunain, thousands of prisoners were captured by the Muslim army. The Prophet waited for many days for their people to come and free them, but they never turned up. The Prophet then returned to Medinah and distributed them among the soldiers. However, after many days had passed, their people showed up. The Prophet said that he had no objection to giving away his share back to them, but as far as the other tribes were concerned, he could only appeal to them. Later, almost all the people surrendered their prisoners when the Prophet, subsequently, offered six camels for each prisoner from the spoils they would obtain in the very next battle. This was enough for them to forfeit their share as well.

- This practical abolition of the institution of slavery continued with full force during the period of the caliphate of the rightly-guided caliphs.

After the Rightly-Guided Caliphs

- Slavery was a unique and complex social and economic problem. Even though the Quran initiated the process of eradication, it required the full support of all layers of society to achieve the desired results.

- Islam expanded from a small city of Medina to many continents in just a few decades.

- After the era of rightly-guided Caliphs, Islam saw a sharp political shift from a democratic style of rule to dictatorship.

- The Islamic society under the rule of dictators and dictators themselves did not wholeheartedly accept the reformation started by Islam.

- The Islamic Jurisprudence, although it accepted the basic principle of freedom of a person, continued to formulate laws related to slavery, which it saw as a form of punishment for disbelief. Much of the jurisprudence on slavery emerged in a patriarchal society politically controlled by despotism and repressive regimes.

- The complexity of the issue of slavery can be easily understood from the fact that it was not until the turn of this century that mankind was actually able to rid itself of this disease.

Sex with Slave-Women

Introduction

- One aspect of slavery that is also 'associated' with Islam is the concept of concubines and the **allowance** of sexual intimacy with them.
- Concubinage refers to the state of a woman or a girl in an ongoing, extra-marital relationship with a man who has captured her through power (usually war).
- The events of the so-called "Islamic State" reignited this debate as they were at the nexus of modern-day concubinage and tried to institutionalize it in the name of Islam.
- Like slavery, Islam does not have the slightest link with concubinage, as this was the practice that existed in the Arab world before the time of Prophet Muhammad.
- In the era of tribal societies, the tribes used to capture women/girls of the enemy and take them as concubines.
- Again, the confusion arose from the fact that Islam did not abolish the institution of slavery, including the practice of concubinage, and adopted a gradual process to abolish it over a period of time (at least that was the intent).
- At best, we can say that Islam **tolerated** this relationship within a household.

Islam's Approach

- As explained earlier, Islam did not abolish the institution of slavery and **tolerated** the extra-marital relationship between the 'owner' and the slave-women.
- Generally, Quran termed sexual relationship outside of marriage as Zina (used for open relationship with multiple partners) but **tolerated** the relationship with concubines and considered it 'legal' during the revelation while on the other hand, it started the process of eradicating this social evil – Quran termed them "women whom your right hand possess" in order to be clear that this relationship is 'allowed' due to the long-held custom of Arabs.
- It must be clear also that Allah **tolerated** this relationship within a house because of the protection that the slave girl would get because of that.
- If Islam had prohibited the custom of having sexual relations with slave girls, then the episodes of sexual harassment in the households would have increased.

- Describing the features of true believers, the Quran said:

وَ الَّذِيۡنَ هُمۡ لِفُرُوۡجِهِمۡ حٰفِظُوۡنَ ۙ اِلَّا عَلٰۤى اَزۡوَاجِهِمۡ اَوۡ مَا مَلَكَتۡ اَيۡمَانُهُمۡ فَاِنَّهُمۡ غَيۡرُ مَلُوۡمِيۡنَ

فَمَنِ ابۡتَغٰى وَرَآءَ ذٰلِكَ فَاُولٰٓئِكَ هُمُ الۡعٰدُوۡنَ

And those who guard their private parts, except from their wives and/or from what 'their right hands possess' because in this matter there is no blame on them. But whoever wishes besides that would be from the transgressors. (Surah Maarij:30-31)

Steps towards freedom

- Out of many steps that Islam adopted towards the freedom of slaves in general, some of them were quite pertinent to slave-women to help them gain the lost dignity.

وَ مَنۡ لَّمۡ يَسۡتَطِعۡ مِنۡكُمۡ طَوۡلًا اَنۡ يَّنۡكِحَ الۡمُحۡصَنٰتِ الۡمُؤۡمِنٰتِ فَمِنۡ مَّا مَلَكَتۡ اَيۡمَانُكُمۡ مِّنۡ فَتَيٰتِكُمُ الۡمُؤۡمِنٰتِ

وَ اللّٰهُ اَعۡلَمُ بِاِيۡمَانِكُمۡ ۚ بَعۡضُكُمۡ مِّنۡۢ بَعۡضٍ ۚ فَانۡكِحُوۡهُنَّ بِاِذۡنِ اَهۡلِهِنَّ وَ اٰتُوۡهُنَّ اُجُوۡرَهُنَّ بِالۡمَعۡرُوۡفِ مُحۡصَنٰتٍ

غَيۡرَ مُسٰفِحٰتٍ وَّ لَا مُتَّخِذٰتِ اَخۡدَانٍ

And if any one of you does not have the means wherewith to wed free believing women, he may wed believing girls from among those whom your right hands possess: and Allah has full knowledge about your faith. You are one from another: so, wed them with the permission of their owners, and give them their dowers, according to the norms; [the only condition is that] they should be kept chaste, neither being lustful, nor taking paramours. (4:25)

وَ اَنۡكِحُوا الۡاَيَامٰى مِنۡكُمۡ وَ الصّٰلِحِيۡنَ مِنۡ عِبَادِكُمۡ وَ اِمَآئِكُمۡ ؕ اِنۡ يَّكُوۡنُوۡا فُقَرَآءَ يُغۡنِهِمُ اللّٰهُ مِنۡ فَضۡلِهٖ ؕ وَ اللّٰهُ وَاسِعٌ عَلِيۡمٌ

And marry those among you who are single and those who are fit among your male slaves and your female slaves; if they are poor, Allah will give them provisions out of His grace; and Allah is Ample-giving, Knowing. (24:32)

وَ الَّذِيۡنَ يَبۡتَغُوۡنَ الۡكِتٰبَ مِمَّا مَلَكَتۡ اَيۡمَانُكُمۡ فَكَاتِبُوۡهُمۡ اِنۡ عَلِمۡتُمۡ فِيۡهِمۡ خَيۡرًا ۖ وَّ اٰتُوۡهُمۡ مِّنۡ مَّالِ اللّٰهِ الَّذِىۡۤ اٰتٰىكُمۡ

And from among your slaves, those who seek Mukatibat, do so with them if you know they are good (and they have the capability), and (believers) give them from wealth that God has given you. (24:33)

The practice of Prophet Muhammad

- Living in a tribal society where slavery was rampant, the Prophet was given slaves as a gift, and he freed all of them – some of them refused to leave him and stayed with him like Zayd bin Haritha.
- One slave lady, Maria Qibtiyyah, was sent as a gift from the ruler of Egypt to the Prophet when the Prophet invited him to Islam. The Prophet kept her as a slave and had sexual relations with her as per the social norms of that time. The scholars presented the following reasons for his action:
    - He accepted her because refusing a gift from a ruler was considered socially awkward at the time.
    - God revealed a special law for the marriages of Prophet Muhammad in the Quran, which allowed him to marry certain types of women. After that, he was barred from marrying any more women, so marrying Maria was not an option.
    - All the wives of the Prophet were given a choice to leave Prophet Muhammad before this special law of marriages for Prophet Muhammad was announced. They were asked to remain in their house under very protective conditions. This could no longer be offered to Maria.
    - Since he was advocating for uplifting the rights and dignity of slaves in society, he used this opportunity to demonstrate how slave women should be treated in the household.

Few Key Points

- In the old days, when women were captured in wars, one of two things used to happen with them:
    - If they can escape, they become prostitutes to feed themselves in the new place they were brought to.
    - Their captors would force them to prostitute and earn money from them.
- The most appropriate way of putting this is that having sexual relations with slave-women was a practice before Islam, and Islam **tolerated** it as part of the process of abolition.
- Even after all the steps taken by Islam to free slaves, a lot of slaves refused to leave the homes they were living in, as they had no means to survive outside of their master's house.
- All the steps that Islam took that were necessary to abolish this practice were directed towards the reintegration of the slaves into society and making them dignified and productive members of society.
- After Mukatibat, the Quran encouraged people to help slaves stand on their feet if they decide to go on their own in society and not leave them vulnerable.

Examples from Ahadith

إِذَا أَدَّبَ الرَّجُلُ أَمَتَهُ فَأَحْسَنَ تَأْدِيبَهَا وَعَلَّمَهَا فَأَحْسَنَ تَعْلِيمَهَا ثُمَّ أَعْتَقَهَا فَتَزَوَّجَهَا كَانَ لَهُ أَجْرَانِ

If a man teaches his servant girl good manners, educates her in the best manner, then emancipates her and marries her, he will have a double reward.
Source: Sahih al Bukhari 3262, Grade: Muttafaqun Alayhi

https://www.abuaminaelias.com/islam-and-concubines/

Q & A and Discussion

Chapter 14

Position of Islam on Fine Arts

This chapter discusses the position of Islam on Music and other art forms like pictures, etc. We will dive deeper into what the Quran and Sunnah say about it and how Ahadith related to them must be understood.

Music

Introduction

 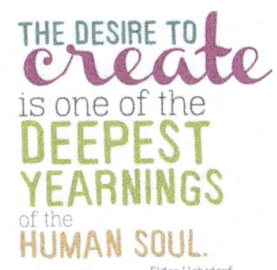

- The issue of music, theatre, portraiture, and other forms of fine art in Islam is somewhat controversial.
- It is generally believed that Islam's attitude towards all forms of fine art is not very encouraging.
- People are confused that if music is food for the soul and art is the best form of self-expression human beings are ever endowed with, then why are they considered prohibited in Islam?
- To settle this confusion in their minds, people have created this self-made dichotomy in music and art by calling it Islamic vs non-Islamic music or Islamic vs non-Islamic art.
- The tendency of contemporary Islamic scholarship is that if the general usage of something in society is negative or harmful, then, as a precaution, they render that thing prohibited in order for people to stay away from it.
- However, when it comes to declaring something allowed or prohibited in the Shariah of Islam, this is not a desirable attitude and must be avoided at all costs.

General understanding

- The general perception is that "there is a consensus among all Muslim Jurists that music and other forms of fine art are forbidden in the Shariah of Islam".
- A few verses from the Quran are cited as evidence, but many Ahadith on the fine arts suggest that Islam discourages or disapproves of the fine arts.
- There is a band of views among scholarly circles when it comes to the prohibition of fine arts:
    1. Some consider it completely forbidden in all forms.
    2. Some only forbid singing with musical instruments and drawing living beings (humans, angels, etc.).
    3. Some allow only specific musical instruments, like 'Duff' (tambourine), and specific genres of music, like "Qawwali," to suit their school of thought.

- The reason for this confusion and range of views is that there is no single statement in the Quran or Ahadith that categorically forbids fine arts or music specifically.
- Scholars' view of the prohibition of fine arts is only an indirect inference from some of the comments made by Prophet Muhammad regarding music and pictures in Ahadith.

Verses Presented as Evidence

- In the absence of any direct evidence from the Quran on the prohibition of Music and fine arts in general, the indirect evidence is inferred from the following verses in the Quran:

وَ مِنَ النَّاسِ مَنْ يَّشْتَرِیْ لَهْوَ الْحَدِیْثِ لِیُضِلَّ عَنْ سَبِیْلِ اللهِ بِغَیْرِ عِلْمٍ

And there are people who are always ready to buy in frivolous matters to lead people astray from the path of God without knowledge (Quran 31:6)

Analysis: The phrase "*lahw al Hadees*" is applied to anything that people can engage in such a way that they lose the sense of purpose and time – this is applicable to discourses, music, games, sports, poetry, or any recreational activity that has no purpose or objective (adopted for pastime). The Quran addresses such activity in relation to the guidance it provides to the people of Quraysh.

وَ اسْتَفْزِزْ مَنِ اسْتَطَعْتَ مِنْهُمْ بِصَوْتِکَ

And beguile whoever you can among them with your loud noise (Quran 17:64)

Analysis: The context of these verses refers to the situation when Satan has decided to disobey God and threatens to misguide people. On that occasion, God told him to go ahead and misguide people by creating a nuisance to God's guidance, such as the Quran.

وَ الَّذِیْنَ لَا یَشْهَدُوْنَ الزُّوْرَ ۙ وَ اِذَا مَرُّوْا بِاللَّغْوِ مَرُّوْا کِرَامًا

(and the Slaves of Ar Rahman) are those who do not get involved in falsehood, and when pass by vain things, they move on with dignity (Quran 25:72)

Analysis: The context of this verse is the discussion of the attributes of a believer. In that context, God is talking about two of their attributes. They do not get involved in falsehoods (of any kind), and when they pass by idle talk or futile or immoral acts, they pass by with dignity without getting involved in that, too.

اَفَمِنْ هٰذَا الْحَدِيْثِ تَعْجَبُوْنَ وَ تَضْحَكُوْنَ وَ لَا تَبْكُوْنَ ۙ وَ اَنْتُمْ سٰمِدُوْنَ

So, does this statement sound strange to you? Make you laugh and not cry, while you are indulged in amusement?   (Quran 53:59-61)

Analysis: The context of these verses is when God admonishes the disbelievers for their behavior towards this Quran. In that context, God is showing them their attitude, which is outright dismissive when it comes to the Quran. They prefer vain discourses, amusements, and futile acts over God's words.

The General Principle about prohibitions

- When it comes to interpreting Shariah for the allowance or forbiddance of something, the following principles must be considered:

  1. It is ONLY the Quran and Sunnah that can categorically prohibit something in Islam. Hadith only elaborates on that prohibition or states the corollary of a principle already mentioned in the Quran and Sunnah. Hadith, as a historical record of the Prophet's life, cannot serve as an independent source for Shariah.

  2. If a particular matter or application of a principle is mentioned in a hadith, then it is necessary to collect all the Ahadith related to that topic and paint a complete picture of it instead of relying on one single instance of it. Sometimes, a single incident is reported by multiple narrators, with differences in the details. All narrations must be looked at to see the full picture.

Quran on Fine Arts

- From the verses on the last slide, one can easily conclude the following:

  1. There is not a single verse in the Quran that categorically prohibits music or any other form of art the same way it does, for example, alcohol or the meat of a pig, etc.

  2. The words used in these verses cover everything that is considered vain, futile, fruitless, useless, worthless, etc. This could be talk, discourse, poetry, sport, games, events, socialization, or even something related to art like music. If one must use these verses as the basis for prohibition, then all these categories must be prohibited. There is nothing specific to music or fine arts in these verses.

  3. God called something futile or worthless when people are engaged in it against the message of God and the Quran. That was the motive of Quryash. They used idle talk, discourses, poetry, music, social gatherings, and many such things to sway people away from the Quran. This situation can make even a permissible thing prohibited at that moment.

- Contrary to what people have understood from the Quran, it praises the voice of Prophet Dawood for singing hymns, with which mountains and birds used to sing along (38:18-19).
- When the Quran spoke of the power and miracles of Prophet Suleiman, it mentioned that the Jinns under his control would make large statues in his palaces for beautification (34:13).

Foundations for Prohibition in the Quran

- The Quran did not leave the matter of prohibitions to interpretation or inference. When it comes to other prohibitions in Shariah, its language is very clear and to the point. It is not possible that the Quran intended to prohibit music but used vague language in doing so. This is not the way God speaks.
- Since music and fine arts are related to morality, any prohibitions related to music or fine arts, in general, must be looked at in the light of these guiding principles.

Prohibitions in the Quran	
Food	**Morals**
<ul><li>The general principle is that all pure food is permissible.</li><li>Verses related to prohibitions are explicitly given in the Quran, leaving no room for inference.</li></ul>	The guiding principles for moral prohibitions are listed in Surah Aaraaf, verse 33:<ul><li>Sexual immoralities hidden or open.</li><li>Usurping other people's rights.</li><li>Trespassing and excessive behavior.</li><li>Associating partners with God.</li><li>Lying to God about things which He did not say.</li></ul>

Analyzing Ahadith

If all the Ahadith are examined in the light of the guiding principles mentioned in the Quran about immoral behavior, the following can be concluded:

1. None of the Ahadith categorically prohibit music or any other form of fine art (examples are given later).
2. The comments of the Prophet about music are mixed. Some Ahadith praise music, some encourage it on certain occasions, some warn against excessive indulgence, and some condemn it due to the immoralities associated with it.
3. In other words, it is the use of these fine arts that is discussed, not the direct prohibition.
4. Some of the late-night gatherings of music in Medinah were objectionable because of lewdness, consumption of alcohol, and involvement of slave-girls in dance and other immoral activities.

5. Music was primarily associated with these late-night gatherings.
6. Pictures and statues were condemned due to their association with polytheistic beliefs and practices.

Music: Hadith 1

Hussain ibn Ali reported that Ali said: "From among the spoils of Badr, a she-camel was given to me as my share. Besides her, the Prophet also gave me another she-camel from [the gains of] Khums. When my marriage was arranged with Fatimah, the daughter of the Prophet, I made a deal with a goldsmith from the tribe of Qaynuqah to accompany me in bringing a special type of grass, loading it onto the camels. By selling this grass to the goldsmiths, I wanted to throw my Walimah. For this, I arranged ropes and a pack saddle for my she-camels. These camels were in the house of a member of the Ansar tribe. After gathering these things, I went to the camels. I saw that someone had chopped off their humps and taken out their livers by cutting open their stomachs. I could not restrain my tears in this situation. I asked people: 'Who is responsible for this?' They replied: Hamzah ibn Abd al-Muttalib; he is drinking liquor in this house along with many people of the Ansar. A songstress is also present there along with his friends. What happened was that when she sang the following words: "Hamzah! Get up and slay these robust she-camels," he immediately pounced on them with a sword and chopped off their humps, and took out their livers by slicing open their stomachs." (Sahih Bukhari #3781)

Analysis: This hadith paints the picture of the gatherings and shows how these gatherings were a means of stimulating base emotions in people, excessive drinking, and promoting promiscuity. These musical gatherings were discouraged and disallowed later, not because music was forbidden, but because of these.

Music: Hadith 2

Urwah reports that Aishah said: "The Prophet [once] came over to me. On this occasion, two slave-girls were singing songs related to the battle of Buath. He lay down on a bed and turned himself to the other side. [In the meantime], Abu Bakr came along and scolded me [for what was going on] and said: 'Why these devilish musical instruments in the presence of the Prophet?' The Prophet turned and said: 'Leave them alone [and let them sing]. When Abu Bakr got involved in some work, I gestured towards these songstresses to go. So, they went away. This was the day of Eid. (Sahih Bukhari #907)

Analysis: If music were prohibited, there would be no reason to allow it, regardless of the occasion. Not only did he not express any resentment towards the two slave-girls, but he also stopped Abu Bakr from showing any reaction to it, who wanted them to stop singing.

Music: Hadith 3

Al-Rabi bint Maudh said: "When I departed as a bride [to my husband's house], the Prophet came over to me and sat on my bedding the way you are sitting on it. At that moment, our slave-girls were singing an elegy to the martyrs of Badr on a small tambourine. On this occasion, one of the slave-girls, while singing, said the words: 'Present amongst us is the Prophet who knows what is going to happen in the future.' At this, the Prophet said: 'Do not say this, but sing what you were singing before." (Sahih Bukhari #3779)

Analysis: It seems that it was a common practice among Arabs for slave girls and boys to sing on different occasions, and that singing was not an independent or personal art form at that time. In this hadith, slave-girls used a tambourine, but the Prophet did not object to its use.

Music: Hadith 4

Ali said that he heard the Prophet say: I never even intended to get indulged in any of the bad customs and practices of Jahiliyya except on two occasions when God protected me from committing the sin. One time, I was grazing my family's goats with a young Qurayshi friend when I asked him to take care of my goats while I intended to spend the night like other teenagers of my village (usually it's spending the night at places where slave-girls used to sing, people drink, and commit other social evils like fake storytelling, etc.). When I was near the entrance to Makkah, I heard music being played on instruments, including a tambourine. I asked what was going on, and people told me there was a marriage ceremony here. I sat down, started listening to the music, and completely forgot where I was going until sleep overtook me. When I woke up, it was already morning, and the sun was bright. I came back to my friend and told him about this incident. The Prophet said that the same thing happened to me the next night, and I could not attend the night party again, as I got involved in listening to the music at another marriage ceremony until sleep overtook me. I woke up to bright sunshine, and I could not attend the party. (Sahih Ibn Hibban #6272)

Analysis: This hadith clearly shows that the Prophet was protected from the evils of society, namely those night parties involving music. But interestingly, he was protected by God while listening to the music at a marriage ceremony. That concludes that evil was associated with the party, not the music.

For detailed analysis of all the Ahadith, please watch all the programs on music:
https://www.youtube.com/watch?v=CKbgZ8Fv3Do

Pictures/Statue: Hadith

The following Ahadith are usually presented as evidence for the prohibition of pictures and statues:

Abdullah ibn Umar reports from the Prophet: "Indeed, creators of such pictures will be punished on the Day of Judgement, and it would be said to them: 'Inject life in what you have created.'" (Sahih Bukhari #5607)

Abdullah ibn Masood reported that the Prophet said: "Those who will be most severely punished by God on the Day of Resurrection will be the image-makers." (Sahih Bukhari 10/382)

Abu Hurairah reported that the Prophet said: "God said: 'Who does more wrong than the one who tries to create something like My creation? Let him create a grain of wheat or a kernel of corn.'" (Sahih Bukhari 10/385).

Ali said: "Shall I not send you on the same mission as the Messenger of God sent me? Do not leave any elevated grave without leveling it, and do not leave any picture in any house without erasing it." (Al Nisaai)

Ibn Abbas reported that the Prophet said: "Every image-maker will be in the Fire, and for every image that he made, a soul will be created for him, which will be punished in the Fire." Ibn Abbas said: "If you must do that, make pictures of trees and other inanimate objects." (Sahih Muslim 3/1871)

Pictures/Statue: Analysis
- Looking at all the Ahadith related to pictures/statues, it is quite clear that the stance of Islam on this issue has been grossly misunderstood.
- At the time of the Prophet Muhammad, the entire Arabian Peninsula was engaged in polytheism and idolatry, and they made portraits and statues of idols, including angels they worshiped. The people of Arabia regarded them as deities designated by God. God sent Prophet Muhammad to eradicate polytheism from its roots and hence his stern stance on pictures and statues, especially of living beings.
- The Quran regards monotheism as the fundamental article of faith, and that's why only pictures and statues, which cultivate sentiments of worship (for example, of angels, forefathers, scholars, saints, etc.) in people, are prohibited.
- If these Ahadith are carefully studied, the words which cannot be missed are "such pictures" and "these pictures", which point only to a certain type of portraits and not to all forms.
- One can conclude from these Ahadith and explanation that Islam DOES NOT prohibit pictures and portraits in its absolute sense, and it's the use of that fine art that is questioned, not the art itself.

Concluding Remarks

- When it comes to moral issues, the principles of determining Haram (prohibited) have been outlined in this verse of Surah Aaraaf:

قُلْ إِنَّمَا حَرَّمَ رَبِّيَ الْفَوَاحِشَ مَا ظَهَرَ مِنْهَا وَ مَا بَطَنَ وَ الْاِثْمَ وَ الْبَغْىَ بِغَيْرِ الْحَقِّ وَ اَنْ تُشْرِكُوا بِاللهِ مَا لَمْ يُنَزِّلْ بِهٖ سُلْطٰنًا وَّ اَنْ تَقُوْلُوْا عَلَى اللهِ مَا لَا تَعْلَمُوْنَ

Say: My Lord has **only** prohibited sexual immorality, whether open or hidden, usurping other people's rights, trespassing, and excessive behavior towards others, associating with partners with God, lying to God about things which you have no knowledge of. (Aaraaf:33)

- God has stressed (by using the word "ONLY") that only these are the things that have been forbidden in Islam. Consequently, whatever things we would find prohibited in Islam have one or more of the above elements in them. Apart from these, everything else is lawful. Hence, if we encounter a new practice and need to decide whether it is prohibited, we must analyze it under the above-mentioned principles.

- If we now look at fine arts in the light of this verse, we can appreciate that if any form of fine arts is used for spreading sexual immorality, shirk, dishonoring, and insulting fellow human beings, etc., it will be considered disliked and prohibited in the religion of Islam.

- However, if someone decides not to listen to music because of the moral degradation society has witnessed across all forms of fine art, that will be their personal decision. However, this is different from considering something prohibited in religion, as the right to prohibit something belongs only to Allah and His messenger.

Q & A and Discussion

Position of Islam on Fine Arts

This chapter discusses the position of Islam on Music and other art forms like pictures, etc. We will dive deeper into what the Quran and Sunnah say about it and how Ahadith related to them must be understood.

Music

Introduction

THE DESIRE TO *create* is one of the DEEPEST YEARNINGS of the HUMAN SOUL.
Elder Uchtdorf

- The issue of music, theatre, portraiture, and other forms of fine art in Islam is somewhat controversial.
- It is generally believed that Islam's attitude towards all forms of fine art is not very encouraging.
- People are confused that if music is food for the soul and art is the best form of self-expression human beings are ever endowed with, then why are they considered prohibited in Islam?
- To settle this confusion in their minds, people have created this self-made dichotomy in music and art by calling it Islamic vs non-Islamic music or Islamic vs non-Islamic art.
- The tendency of contemporary Islamic scholarship is that if the general usage of something in society is negative or harmful, then, as a precaution, they render that thing prohibited in order for people to stay away from it.
- However, when it comes to declaring something allowed or prohibited in the Shariah of Islam, this is not a desirable attitude and must be avoided at all costs.

General understanding

- The general perception is that "there is a consensus among all Muslim Jurists that music and other forms of fine art are forbidden in the Shariah of Islam".
- A few verses from the Quran are cited as evidence, but many Ahadith on the fine arts suggest that Islam discourages or disapproves of the fine arts.
- There is a band of views among scholarly circles when it comes to the prohibition of fine arts:
  1. Some consider it completely forbidden in all forms.
  2. Some only forbid singing with musical instruments and drawing living beings (humans, angels, etc.).
  3. Some allow only specific musical instruments, like 'Duff' (tambourine), and specific genres of music, like "Qawwali," to suit their school of thought.

- The reason for this confusion and range of views is that there is no single statement in the Quran or Ahadith that categorically forbids fine arts or music specifically.
- Scholars' view of the prohibition of fine arts is only an indirect inference from some of the comments made by Prophet Muhammad regarding music and pictures in Ahadith.

Verses Presented as Evidence

- In the absence of any direct evidence from the Quran on the prohibition of Music and fine arts in general, the indirect evidence is inferred from the following verses in the Quran:

وَ مِنَ النَّاسِ مَنْ يَّشْتَرِىْ لَهْوَ الْحَدِيْثِ لِيُضِلَّ عَنْ سَبِيْلِ اللهِ بِغَيْرِ عِلْمٍ

And there are people who are always ready to buy in frivolous matters to lead people astray from the path of God without knowledge (Quran 31:6)

Analysis: The phrase "*lahw al Hadees*" is applied to anything that people can engage in such a way that they lose the sense of purpose and time – this is applicable to discourses, music, games, sports, poetry, or any recreational activity that has no purpose or objective (adopted for pastime). The Quran addresses such activity in relation to the guidance it provides to the people of Quraysh.

وَ اسْتَفْزِزْ مَنِ اسْتَطَعْتَ مِنْهُمْ بِصَوْتِكَ

And beguile whoever you can among them with your loud noise (Quran 17:64)

Analysis: The context of these verses refers to the situation when Satan has decided to disobey God and threatens to misguide people. On that occasion, God told him to go ahead and misguide people by creating a nuisance to God's guidance, such as the Quran.

وَ الَّذِيْنَ لَا يَشْهَدُوْنَ الزُّوْرَ ۙ وَ اِذَا مَرُّوْا بِاللَّغْوِ مَرُّوْا كِرَامًا

(and the Slaves of Ar Rahman) are those who do not get involved in falsehood, and when pass by vain things, they move on with dignity (Quran 25:72)

Analysis: The context of this verse is the discussion of the attributes of a believer. In that context, God is talking about two of their attributes. They do not get involved in falsehoods (of any kind), and when they pass by idle talk or futile or immoral acts, they pass by with dignity without getting involved in that, too.

اَفَمِنْ هٰذَا الْحَدِيْثِ تَعْجَبُوْنَ وَ تَضْحَكُوْنَ وَ لَا تَبْكُوْنَ ۙ وَ اَنْتُمْ سٰمِدُوْنَ

So, does this statement sound strange to you? Make you laugh and not cry, while you are indulged in amusement? (Quran 53:59-61)

Analysis: The context of these verses is when God admonishes the disbelievers for their behavior towards this Quran. In that context, God is showing them their attitude, which is outright dismissive when it comes to the Quran. They prefer vain discourses, amusements, and futile acts over God's words.

The General Principle about prohibitions

- When it comes to interpreting Shariah for the allowance or forbiddance of something, the following principles must be considered:
  1. It is ONLY the Quran and Sunnah that can categorically prohibit something in Islam. Hadith only elaborates on that prohibition or states the corollary of a principle already mentioned in the Quran and Sunnah. Hadith, as a historical record of the Prophet's life, cannot serve as an independent source for Shariah.
  2. If a particular matter or application of a principle is mentioned in a hadith, then it is necessary to collect all the Ahadith related to that topic and paint a complete picture of it instead of relying on one single instance of it. Sometimes, a single incident is reported by multiple narrators, with differences in the details. All narrations must be looked at to see the full picture.

Quran on Fine Arts

- From the verses on the last slide, one can easily conclude the following:
  1. There is not a single verse in the Quran that categorically prohibits music or any other form of art the same way it does, for example, alcohol or the meat of a pig, etc.
  2. The words used in these verses cover everything that is considered vain, futile, fruitless, useless, worthless, etc. This could be talk, discourse, poetry, sport, games, events, socialization, or even something related to art like music. If one must use these verses as the basis for prohibition, then all these categories must be prohibited. There is nothing specific to music or fine arts in these verses.
  3. God called something futile or worthless when people are engaged in it against the message of God and the Quran. That was the motive of Quryash. They used idle talk, discourses, poetry, music, social gatherings, and many such things to sway people away from the Quran. This situation can make even a permissible thing prohibited at that moment.

- Contrary to what people have understood from the Quran, it praises the voice of Prophet Dawood for singing hymns, with which mountains and birds used to sing along (38:18-19).
- When the Quran spoke of the power and miracles of Prophet Suleiman, it mentioned that the Jinns under his control would make large statues in his palaces for beautification (34:13).

Foundations for Prohibition in the Quran

- The Quran did not leave the matter of prohibitions to interpretation or inference. When it comes to other prohibitions in Shariah, its language is very clear and to the point. It is not possible that the Quran intended to prohibit music but used vague language in doing so. This is not the way God speaks.
- Since music and fine arts are related to morality, any prohibitions related to music or fine arts, in general, must be looked at in the light of these guiding principles.

Prohibitions in the Quran	
Food	**Morals**
• The general principle is that all pure food is permissible. • Verses related to prohibitions are explicitly given in the Quran, leaving no room for inference.	The guiding principles for moral prohibitions are listed in Surah Aaraaf, verse 33: • Sexual immoralities hidden or open. • Usurping other people's rights. • Trespassing and excessive behavior. • Associating partners with God. • Lying to God about things which He did not say.

Analyzing Ahadith

If all the Ahadith are examined in the light of the guiding principles mentioned in the Quran about immoral behavior, the following can be concluded:

1. None of the Ahadith categorically prohibit music or any other form of fine art (examples are given later).
2. The comments of the Prophet about music are mixed. Some Ahadith praise music, some encourage it on certain occasions, some warn against excessive indulgence, and some condemn it due to the immoralities associated with it.
3. In other words, it is the use of these fine arts that is discussed, not the direct prohibition.
4. Some of the late-night gatherings of music in Medinah were objectionable because of lewdness, consumption of alcohol, and involvement of slave-girls in dance and other immoral activities.

5. Music was primarily associated with these late-night gatherings.
6. Pictures and statues were condemned due to their association with polytheistic beliefs and practices.

Music: Hadith 1

Hussain ibn Ali reported that Ali said: "From among the spoils of Badr, a she-camel was given to me as my share. Besides her, the Prophet also gave me another she-camel from [the gains of] Khums. When my marriage was arranged with Fatimah, the daughter of the Prophet, I made a deal with a goldsmith from the tribe of Qaynuqah to accompany me in bringing a special type of grass, loading it onto the camels. By selling this grass to the goldsmiths, I wanted to throw my Walimah. For this, I arranged ropes and a pack saddle for my she-camels. These camels were in the house of a member of the Ansar tribe. After gathering these things, I went to the camels. I saw that someone had chopped off their humps and taken out their livers by cutting open their stomachs. I could not restrain my tears in this situation. I asked people: 'Who is responsible for this?' They replied: Hamzah ibn Abd al-Muttalib; he is drinking liquor in this house along with many people of the Ansar. A songstress is also present there along with his friends. What happened was that when she sang the following words: "Hamzah! Get up and slay these robust she-camels," he immediately pounced on them with a sword and chopped off their humps, and took out their livers by slicing open their stomachs." (Sahih Bukhari #3781)

Analysis: This hadith paints the picture of the gatherings and shows how these gatherings were a means of stimulating base emotions in people, excessive drinking, and promoting promiscuity. These musical gatherings were discouraged and disallowed later, not because music was forbidden, but because of these.

Music: Hadith 2

Urwah reports that Aishah said: "The Prophet [once] came over to me. On this occasion, two slave-girls were singing songs related to the battle of Buath. He lay down on a bed and turned himself to the other side. [In the meantime], Abu Bakr came along and scolded me [for what was going on] and said: 'Why these devilish musical instruments in the presence of the Prophet?' The Prophet turned and said: 'Leave them alone [and let them sing]. When Abu Bakr got involved in some work, I gestured towards these songstresses to go. So, they went away. This was the day of Eid. (Sahih Bukhari #907)

Analysis: If music were prohibited, there would be no reason to allow it, regardless of the occasion. Not only did he not express any resentment towards the two slave-girls, but he also stopped Abu Bakr from showing any reaction to it, who wanted them to stop singing.

Music: Hadith 3

Al-Rabi bint Maudh said: "When I departed as a bride [to my husband's house], the Prophet came over to me and sat on my bedding the way you are sitting on it. At that moment, our slave-girls were singing an elegy to the martyrs of Badr on a small tambourine. On this occasion, one of the slave-girls, while singing, said the words: 'Present amongst us is the Prophet who knows what is going to happen in the future.' At this, the Prophet said: 'Do not say this, but sing what you were singing before." (Sahih Bukhari #3779)

Analysis: It seems that it was a common practice among Arabs for slave girls and boys to sing on different occasions, and that singing was not an independent or personal art form at that time. In this hadith, slave-girls used a tambourine, but the Prophet did not object to its use.

Music: Hadith 4

Ali said that he heard the Prophet say: I never even intended to get indulged in any of the bad customs and practices of Jahiliyya except on two occasions when God protected me from committing the sin. One time, I was grazing my family's goats with a young Qurayshi friend when I asked him to take care of my goats while I intended to spend the night like other teenagers of my village (usually it's spending the night at places where slave-girls used to sing, people drink, and commit other social evils like fake storytelling, etc.). When I was near the entrance to Makkah, I heard music being played on instruments, including a tambourine. I asked what was going on, and people told me there was a marriage ceremony here. I sat down, started listening to the music, and completely forgot where I was going until sleep overtook me. When I woke up, it was already morning, and the sun was bright. I came back to my friend and told him about this incident. The Prophet said that the same thing happened to me the next night, and I could not attend the night party again, as I got involved in listening to the music at another marriage ceremony until sleep overtook me. I woke up to bright sunshine, and I could not attend the party. (Sahih Ibn Hibban #6272)

Analysis: This hadith clearly shows that the Prophet was protected from the evils of society, namely those night parties involving music. But interestingly, he was protected by God while listening to the music at a marriage ceremony. That concludes that evil was associated with the party, not the music.

For detailed analysis of all the Ahadith, please watch all the programs on music:
https://www.youtube.com/watch?v=CKbgZ8Fv3Do

Pictures/Statue: Hadith

The following Ahadith are usually presented as evidence for the prohibition of pictures and statues:

Abdullah ibn Umar reports from the Prophet: "Indeed, creators of such pictures will be punished on the Day of Judgement, and it would be said to them: 'Inject life in what you have created.'" (Sahih Bukhari #5607)

Abdullah ibn Masood reported that the Prophet said: "Those who will be most severely punished by God on the Day of Resurrection will be the image-makers." (Sahih Bukhari 10/382)

Abu Hurairah reported that the Prophet said: "God said: 'Who does more wrong than the one who tries to create something like My creation? Let him create a grain of wheat or a kernel of corn.'" (Sahih Bukhari 10/385).

Ali said: "Shall I not send you on the same mission as the Messenger of God sent me? Do not leave any elevated grave without leveling it, and do not leave any picture in any house without erasing it." (Al Nisaai)

Ibn Abbas reported that the Prophet said: "Every image-maker will be in the Fire, and for every image that he made, a soul will be created for him, which will be punished in the Fire." Ibn Abbas said: "If you must do that, make pictures of trees and other inanimate objects." (Sahih Muslim 3/1871)

Pictures/Statue: Analysis

- Looking at all the Ahadith related to pictures/statues, it is quite clear that the stance of Islam on this issue has been grossly misunderstood.
- At the time of the Prophet Muhammad, the entire Arabian Peninsula was engaged in polytheism and idolatry, and they made portraits and statues of idols, including angels they worshiped. The people of Arabia regarded them as deities designated by God. God sent Prophet Muhammad to eradicate polytheism from its roots and hence his stern stance on pictures and statues, especially of living beings.
- The Quran regards monotheism as the fundamental article of faith, and that's why only pictures and statues, which cultivate sentiments of worship (for example, of angels, forefathers, scholars, saints, etc.) in people, are prohibited.
- If these Ahadith are carefully studied, the words which cannot be missed are "such pictures" and "these pictures", which point only to a certain type of portraits and not to all forms.
- One can conclude from these Ahadith and explanation that Islam DOES NOT prohibit pictures and portraits in its absolute sense, and it's the use of that fine art that is questioned, not the art itself.

Concluding Remarks

- When it comes to moral issues, the principles of determining Haram (prohibited) have been outlined in this verse of Surah Aaraaf:

قُلْ اِنَّمَا حَرَّمَ رَبِّيَ الْفَوَاحِشَ مَا ظَهَرَ مِنْهَا وَ مَا بَطَنَ وَ الْاِثْمَ وَ الْبَغْىَ بِغَيْرِ الْحَقِّ وَ اَنْ تُشْرِكُوْا بِاللّٰهِ مَا لَمْ يُنَزِّلْ بِهٖ سُلْطٰنًا وَّ اَنْ تَقُوْلُوْا عَلَى اللّٰهِ مَا لَا تَعْلَمُوْنَ

Say: My Lord has **only** prohibited sexual immorality, whether open or hidden, usurping other people's rights, trespassing, and excessive behavior towards others, associating with partners with God, lying to God about things which you have no knowledge of. (Aaraaf:33)

- God has stressed (by using the word "ONLY") that only these are the things that have been forbidden in Islam. Consequently, whatever things we would find prohibited in Islam have one or more of the above elements in them. Apart from these, everything else is lawful. Hence, if we encounter a new practice and need to decide whether it is prohibited, we must analyze it under the above-mentioned principles.

- If we now look at fine arts in the light of this verse, we can appreciate that if any form of fine arts is used for spreading sexual immorality, shirk, dishonoring, and insulting fellow human beings, etc., it will be considered disliked and prohibited in the religion of Islam.

- However, if someone decides not to listen to music because of the moral degradation society has witnessed across all forms of fine art, that will be their personal decision. However, this is different from considering something prohibited in religion, as the right to prohibit something belongs only to Allah and His messenger.

Q & A and Discussion

Chapter 15

Keeping Dogs

This chapter discusses Islam's stance on keeping pets, especially dogs, as some Ahadith seem to prohibit keeping dogs.

Keeping Dogs

Introduction

- Muslims' traditional view of dogs makes both Muslims and non-Muslims think that Islam views dogs as a ritually impure, filthy, and evil animal.
- Non-Muslims, seeing a Muslim's reaction to dogs, are given the impression that Muslims fear and hate dogs.
- It will be hard to believe that the first Muslims did not keep dogs, since they had large flocks of sheep and goats (their means of survival) and also went out on hunting expeditions (for both sport and food).
- Dogs have also been used as guards, as in those times, the concept of state-provided safety and security was in its infancy.
- However, humans did not always keep dogs solely for companionship, love, and affection; this is a newer concept, born of the needs of Western societies.
- We all agree that a well-trained dog can be a source of joy and happiness, but the real issue arises from the uncleanliness associated with dogs and the closeness or attachment the owner has to the dog in his/her home.

General Understanding

- Due to certain Ahadith, it is generally understood that Muslims must not keep dogs as they are unclean, keeping them takes away from their good deeds, and also, angels do not enter their house.
- The following Ahadith are presented:

طَهُورُ إِنَاءِ أَحَدِكُمْ إِذَا وَلَغَ فِيهِ الْكَلْبُ أَنْ يَغْسِلَهُ سَبْعَ مَرَّاتٍ أُولَاهُنَّ بِالتُّرَابِ

"When a dog laps the water in a vessel belonging to any of you, he must wash it seven times, using earth the first time." (Sahih Muslim)

لَا تَدْخُلُ الْمَلَائِكَةُ بَيْتًا فِيهِ كَلْبٌ وَلَا صُورَةُ تَمَاثِيلَ

"The angels do not enter a house in which there is a dog, nor an image in a likeness (living soul)." (Sahih Bukhari #3225)

من اقتنى كلبًا ليس بكلب صيد، ولا ماشية ولا أرض، فإنه ينقص من أجره قيراطان كل يوم

"Whoever holds a dog for any reason other than to guard his property (lands) or his flock of sheep, his good deeds equal to two Qirat will be deducted every day." (Riyad As Saliheen # 1689)

- Some Muslims are also of the opinion that the saliva of a dog breaks the Wudu, and also that prayers are not accepted in their presence.

Analysis of the general understanding

- In order to understand the issue in detail, the following must be looked at:
  - The Quran's view on dogs.
  - The understanding of the Narratives related to dogs.
  - Interacting with dogs – the right attitude.

Quran's view on dogs

- The Quran did not discuss it as a topic, but various examples suggest a completely different view of what Muslims have understood.
- For e.g., the Quran appreciates the dog owned by the People of the Cave and how it sat outside the cave guarding it watchfully.
- It is assumed that angels must be coming into the cave and turning their sides while they slept for 100s of years, as described in the Quran.
- The Quran also allowed Muslims to eat from the meat of the prey that was held by a trained dog when it was let loose on the prey after taking the name of God.

قُلْ أُحِلَّ لَكُمُ الطَّيِّبَٰتُ ۙ وَ مَا عَلَّمْتُم مِّنَ الْجَوَارِحِ مُكَلِّبِينَ تُعَلِّمُونَهُنَّ مِمَّا عَلَّمَكُمُ اللَّهُ ۖ فَكُلُوا مِمَّآ أَمْسَكْنَ عَلَيْكُمْ وَ اذْكُرُوا اسْمَ اللَّهِ عَلَيْهِ

Say, all pure things are allowed and also of what you have taught the beasts (dogs) and birds of prey, training them to hunt, you teach them of what Allah has taught you, so eat of that which they catch for you and (before releasing the animal) mention the name of Allah over it (Maidah: 4)

- The verse suggests that their catch is not considered impure in any way and is considered pure for eating; otherwise, extra instructions must be given to cleanse the meat.

1 – Uncleanliness Issue

- This issue, highlighted in the hadith, must be viewed in light of the fact that dogs can carry harmful or infectious diseases in their saliva, as can some other pets; also, if they are not properly trained, they can defecate all over the house.
- The Prophet's instructions regarding washing utensils licked by a dog multiple times with water and earth/soil are due to this disease or uncleanliness, because the dog was a stray (this may also apply to cats) and not a matter of religious or ritual cleanliness.
- That's why the Maliki Fiqh views it as commonsense advice to prevent the spread of disease.
- The solution to this problem is to:
  - Train the dogs to keep their living area clean.
  - Get all the required vaccinations done regularly as recommended by the veterinarians.

2 – Angels do not enter the house

- Angels possess a very refined personality, especially that of Angel Jibrael, which is very sensitive to impurities, both spiritual (polytheism) and physical (body excretions).
- The narration attributed to the Prophet concerns an incident in which a stray dog defecated under the Prophet's bed or camp while he was unaware. The Prophet was waiting for Jibrael, as he had promised to come the night before. When the Prophet cleaned that area and removed the untrained dog, Jibrael then came and explained the reason for his refusal to enter the house.
- There are multiple narrations related to this incident, and when all the narrations are looked at carefully, it becomes clear that hesitance was due to the untrained nature of the dog and the filth it caused in the house, and also due to the sophisticated personality of Angel Jibrael, who was assigned the duty of bringing the sacred text from God.

3 – Losing the reward of good deeds

- This narration has been completely misunderstood, as it does not talk about keeping dogs but rather "tying or holding dogs" for no reason.
- The directive in this hadith is very much in compliance with the teachings of Islam, which prohibit us from being cruel to all living beings, including animals.
- The wording of the hadith is: "Whoever holds a dog for any reason other than to guard his property (lands) or his flock of sheep, his good deeds equal to two Qirat will be deducted every day." (Riyad As Saliheen # 1689).

- In those times, those were the only two reasons people kept dogs.
- Losing the reward of your deeds if you are being insensitive to animals' rights and their well-being follows the teachings of Islam.
- This may be true for caged birds, also, who we usually keep to entertain ourselves, despite knowing that birds love to live in the open air.

The general philosophy of Islamic Shariah holds that nothing in the Shariah is prohibited or considered disliked without sound reasoning. Since dogs are considered "undesirable" based on some of the narrations, none of these narrations offers any rationale behind this attitude towards dogs. Hence, it was necessary to understand the narrations in the proper context of the events they reported.

Interacting with dogs – the right attitude

- One can conclude from the aforementioned discussions that there is no harm in Muslims petting dogs for whatever reason they want, as long as they are properly trained to keep their homes clean.
- Even if someone does not want to pet a dog for any reason, their attitude towards the dog must be one of love and care, not of fear and hate.
- In societies where stray dogs are abundant, the behavior towards them would be visibly different from societies where dogs are taken care of and properly trained for companionship
- Since Muslims are extra careful about cleanliness, the following steps can be taken to maintain that sense of cleanliness:
  - Keep a separate designated place for prayers, and train the dog not to go there.
  - Train the dog not to lick your food or utensils, and only allow them to eat their designated food in their designated utensils.
  - They can be allowed to sleep in your room on their own designated place.

Q & A and Discussion

Chapter 16

Tattoos and Magic

This chapter discusses Islam's stance on making tattoos on the body and also practices related to magic and other occult sciences.

Position of Islam on Tattoos

Introduction

"My Yemeni great-grandmother had tattoos on her face, which always seemed extraordinary to me." (Yumna Al Arashi)

https://www.itsnicethat.com/articles/yumna-al-arashi-face-photography-internationalwomensday-080318

 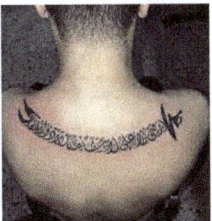

- Tattoos date back many thousands of years and are considered an ancient art form.
- There is a range of opinion among the religious groups of the Abrahamic tradition, including Judaism, Christianity, and Islam.
- The majority of the scholars of all three Abrahamic religions consider it forbidden for many reasons, including "an attempt to change the creation of God".
- Despite various religious decrees in this regard, both Sunni and Shia Muslims have adorned themselves with tattoos of cultural display for centuries, for e.g., Pathans of South/Central Asia are known for tattooing themselves with etchings to deflect the evil eye.
- In recent times, it has been one of the most contentious issues between Muslim children and their parents.
- Another important aspect to consider is what (content) has been etched on your body – it ranges from Allah's name, verses of the Quran, the name of the Prophet, pictures, national symbols, to devilish figures.

General Understanding

- The majority of the Muslim Jurists believe that Tattooing is prohibited in all forms because of two reasons:
  - In the Quran in verse 119 of Surah Nisa, Satan promised God that he would misguide people from the straight path, and one of the ways he would do that those people would make alteration to the creation of God.
  - Also, in Surah Rum, verse 30, God said that it is not allowed to change in God's creation.
  - There are Ahadith in Sahih Bukhari that categorically prohibit tattooing.

لَعَنَهُ اللهُ ۘ وَ قَالَ لَاَتَّخِذَنَّ مِنْ عِبَادِكَ نَصِيبًا مَّفْرُوْضًا

وَّ لَاُضِلَّنَّهُمْ وَ لَاُمَنِّيَنَّهُمْ وَ لَاٰمُرَنَّهُمْ فَلَيُبَتِّكُنَّ اٰذَانَ الْاَنْعَامِ وَ لَاٰمُرَنَّهُمْ فَلَيُغَيِّرُنَّ خَلْقَ اللهِ

Allah has cursed him, and he has already said that 'most certainly I will take an appointed portion from your slaves. And most certainly I will lead them astray and excite in them vain desires, and suggest to them so that they shall slit the ears of the cattle, and most certainly I will suggest to them so that they shall alter Allah's creation. (Surah Nisa:118-119)

فِطْرَتَ اللهِ الَّتِيْ فَطَرَ النَّاسَ عَلَيْهَا ۘ لَا تَبْدِيْلَ لِخَلْقِ اللهِ

Follow the nature (with regards to religion) in which God has created all human beings. No change should be made in the creation of God. (Surah Rum: 30)

Abdullah ibn Masood reports that the Prophet said: "May Allah curse the women who do tattoos and those for whom tattoos are done, those who pluck their eyebrows and those who file their teeth for the purpose of beautification and alter the creation of Allah." (Sahih Bukhari #5587; Sahih Muslim #5538)

Another version from Abdullah bin Masud

`Abdullah (bin Masud) said. "Allah curses those ladies who practice tattooing and those who get themselves tattooed, and those ladies who remove the hair from their faces and those who make artificial spaces between their teeth in order to look more beautiful, whereby they change Allah's creation." His saying reached a lady from Bani Asd called Um Yaqub who came (to `Abdullah) and said, "I have come to know that you have cursed such-and-such (ladies)?" He replied, "Why should I not curse these whom Allah's Messenger has cursed and who are (cursed) in Allah's Book!" Um Yaqub said, "I have read the whole Qur'an, but I did not find in it what you say." He said, "Verily, if you have read it (i.e., the Qur'an), you have found it. Didn't you read: 'And whatsoever the Apostle gives you, take it and whatsoever he forbids you, you abstain (from it). (59.7) She replied, "Yes, I did." He said, "Verily, Allah's Messenger forbade such things." "She said, "But I see your wife doing these things?" He said, "Go and watch her." She went to watch her, but could not see anything to support her statement. On that, he said, "If my wife were as you thought, I would not keep her in my company."

The Prophet cursed the women who practice tattooing and those who seek to be tattooed, the women who remove hair from their faces seeking beautification by changing the creation of Allah. (Al Tirmidhi #2782)

Analysis of the general Understanding

- Any practice considered Haram or prohibited in Islam must have its roots in the general principles outlined in the Quran, specifically Surah Aaraf, verse 33, on prohibition.
- Keeping that guideline in mind, the act of tattooing itself cannot be considered bad, but it's the content or the purpose of the tattoo that makes it prohibited in Islam – this is the same principle that we applied for music, in which it's the use of the music and its content that makes it allowed or prohibited.
- The verses 118-119 of Surah Nisa and 30 of Surah Rum talked about 'changing the creation of God' which is applicable to acts like acts of polytheism (because human beings are created with the concept of one God) or acts in which women try to become men and men try to become women through artificial means or e.g., going through the sex-change surgeries without medical issues or needs.
- Also, these verses came in the context of polytheism and polytheistic acts that Quraysh used to do – people used to have tattoos to save themselves from evil eyes.
- Looking at all the Ahadith related to this subject, it appears that the Prophet of God recited verse 30 of Surah Rum at the end, which clearly indicates that he was alluding to acts of polytheism when he referred to tattooing and similar practices at that time.

Few Key Points

- Not everything should be viewed through the lens of religion; whether one should get a tattoo depends more on personal preference than anything else.
- There is a big cultural element related to tattooing, and one must consider those cultural aspects when getting a tattoo – parents coming from a completely different cultural background might see tattooing as repulsive.
- When getting a tattoo, the following must be kept in mind:
  - It should not be related to any polytheistic or pagan beliefs.
  - It should not violate Islam's moral teachings.
- Some scholars opine that tattoos prevent proper wudu because water cannot penetrate the ink. However, given that tattoos are completely permeable, nothing about tattoos prevents the skin from being cleansed, and thus they do not invalidate wudu.
- If the ink used is not permeable, one should make Wudu before the tattoo is done, and then do Wudu on top of it afterward (same ruling as for nail polish).

Magic & Witchcraft

Introduction

- Magic is real, and it exists in the world that we live in.
- There are different types of magic. One type of magic is what we often see performed in front of an audience and is mostly involved in tricks.
- The other type of magic is the one that is used by some people on other people to harm them physically, emotionally, and in other ways – there are various names for it, like black magic, voodoo, witchcraft, etc.
- Another thing that is closer to the second type of magic is the evil eye – its harmful effects are very similar to those of magic.
- The harmful effects include sickness, fatigue, inability to do daily tasks, depression, anger, and similar issues that will ultimately take away the quality of life.
- Magic belongs to the branch of knowledge that deals with the spiritual domain (or soul) of this world, while Science is all about the knowledge related to the matter and material things of this world.

Occult Sciences

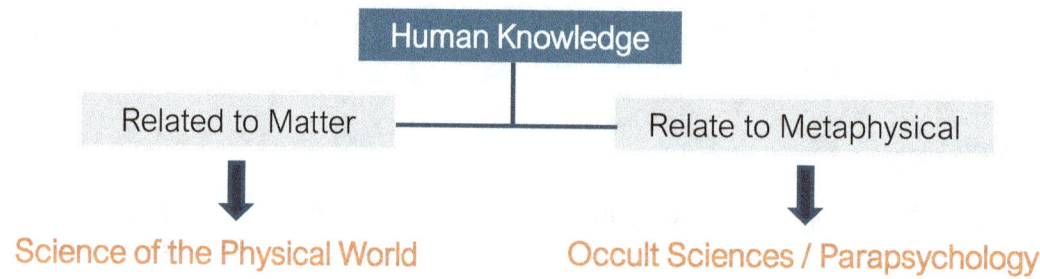

- Magic belongs to the branch of knowledge that deals with the spiritual/soul or metaphysical domain, while Science is all about the knowledge related to the matter and material things of this world.
- Historically, nations and groups of people have sought to understand the intricacies of the metaphysical world and the laws that govern it (also known as the Occult sciences).
- Since it is a very complex domain of knowledge and can be misused against people, it has not been converted into an exact science that can always produce desired results, as in the science of matter.
- People who learned it and mastered it never taught it to the public; they passed it on to their students – some used this knowledge to perform all sorts of magic.

Black magic or Witchcraft

- Black magic or Witchcraft belongs to the Occult sciences.
- People who develop an interest in such sciences often seek a connection to the world of Jinns (the unseen world).
- The knowledge and rules learned in this domain can be used for both beneficial and harmful purposes.

 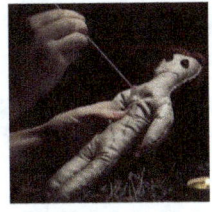

- Since it can significantly affect the human body and psychological behavior, it is often misused to harm people, and when devils or evil Jinns are involved, they exploit the person trying to gain mastery in this field.
- The Quran, in Surah Baqarah (verse 102), mentions such knowledge in the time of Prophet Sulaiman and the Jinns/Devils, who used to teach such sciences (especially black magic) to people for harmful purposes.
- God also sent the two angels (Harut and Marut) to the people of Babylon, who used to teach similar knowledge to the people as a test from God, and most people misused this knowledge, causing separation between husband and wife.

Islam's position on Occult Sciences

- Islam takes a position only on matters that involve a violation of the moral code described in Shariah.
- People use such sciences for various reasons. E.g.,:
    - Telepathy
    - Hypnotism
    - Cure for diseases
    - Dealing with psychological issues
- When using these sciences for any reason, the following must be kept in consideration:
    - It must not involve any practices, beliefs, or writings that contain polytheistic or devilish elements.
    - It must not involve any immoral acts or result in immoral behavior (harming others or taking other people's rights, etc.).
- Generally, these sciences involve people who are not very well-versed and considered quacks in this field, so be careful with that.

Dealing with Black Magic

- If you are a religious person who prays on time, reads the Quran, and makes dua to God on a regular basis, chances are that you will not be affected by black magic.
- However, if someone strongly suspects that the black magic has been cast on him/her, then the following practices are recommended in our Shariah after taking all the necessary medical help:
  - Have a firm belief in God that He is the Most Powerful and Most Capable and in control of everything.
  - Spend more time reciting the Quran and doing prayers.
  - Recite Surah Falaq and Surah Nas as much as possible.
  - Make constant dua and ask God for His protection from such evil practices.

Recommended Duas

قُلْ اَعُوْذُ بِرَبِّ الْفَلَقِ مِنْ شَرِّ مَا خَلَقَ وَ مِنْ شَرِّ غَاسِقٍ اِذَا وَقَبَ
وَ مِنْ شَرِّ النَّفَّثٰتِ فِى الْعُقَدِ وَ مِنْ شَرِّ حَاسِدٍ اِذَا حَسَدَ

Say: "I seek refuge in the Lord of the dawn, from the evil of what He has created; and from the evil of the darkness of the night as it overspreads; and from the evil of the witchcrafts when they blow on knots; and from the evil of the envier when he envies." (Surah Falaq)

قُلْ اَعُوْذُ بِرَبِّ النَّاسِ مَلِكِ النَّاسِ اِلٰهِ النَّاسِ مِنْ شَرِّ الْوَسْوَاسِ الْخَنَّاسِ
الَّذِىْ يُوَسْوِسُ فِىْ صُدُوْرِ النَّاسِ مِنَ الْجِنَّةِ وَ النَّاسِ

Say: "I seek refuge in the Lord of mankind; the King of mankind; the God of mankind; from the evil of the whisperer who withdraws (after whispering); who whispers in the hearts (thinking) of mankind; (he is from) among the Jinns and men." (Surah Nas)

أعِيذُكمـا بكلمات الله التَّامَّة، مِنْ كُلِّ شَيْطان وهـامَّة،
ومِنْ كُلِّ عَيْنٍ لامَّة

U'eethukumaa bikalimaatil-laahit-taam-mati min kulli shaitaanin wa haam-matin, wa min kulli 'ainin laammatin
'I seek refuge for you two with Allaah's perfect words from every Shaytaan (devil) and poisonous creature and every evil eye.'

أَعُوْذُ بِكَلِمَاتِ اللّٰهِ التَّامَّاتِ مِنْ شَرِّ مَا خَلَقَ

A'oothu bi kalimaatil-laahit-taammaati min sharri maa khalaq.
"I seek protection in the perfect words of Allah from every evil that He has created."

Q & A and Discussion

Chapter 17

Pornography and Masturbation

This chapter discusses Islam's stance on some of the challenges that the young generation faces today in the form of watching pornography and self-gratification.

Watching Pornography

Introduction

Internet porn is the new drug	Porn Addiction and Sexual Fantasy is Progressive	A brain on porn is similar to a brain on alcohol

Porn Addiction Turns Watchers into Consumers of the Opposite Sex and Objectifies them (especially women)	Social, health, financial, personality and relationship effects if it becomes an addiction

- The Internet and other technological advances have made pornography more accessible than ever before.
- It's an industry with an enormous business (multi-billion dollars), and knowing the impact of porn addiction on teens, they want more and more of them as consumers – it is an effective tool to keep youths out of morality, decency, and productivity.
- It is a sad reality, but this addition is not limited to unmarried and young people. The surveys suggest that most of its consumers are married.
- Non-Muslims may be behind the industry, but sadly, Muslims are equally consumers of pornography as non-Muslims.
- Everybody understands that adultery is a major sin and must be avoided and prohibited in Islam, but people are confused about watching pornography, as the virtual world of pornography seems hazy.
- Since the Shariah does not address it directly, the scholars of Islam have looked at it from the point of view of 'something that leads to Haram'.

Islam's Position

- Islam's position on this topic is clear at least in the realm of its nature. It's a sin.
- The objective of all the instructions (allowances or prohibitions) in the religion of Islam is Tazkiyah (purification of the self) – it demands that our beliefs and deeds be developed in the right direction to help us attain purification.
- There is a debate about whether watching pornography is technically considered Haram, but scholars have a consensus that it is a sin. Willful violation of this order may equate it with rebellion and can incur grave consequences in the Hereafter.
- When it comes to the prohibition of adultery, the Quran also uses the words "don't even go near adultery," which suggests that a believer should avoid anything that leads to the ultimate prohibition, and one can easily conclude that watching pornography is one of those acts.

- The sin of adultery is at the core of prohibition, but it has its gravitational field that, if you go in, the chances are that you will fall into it, so a believer should avoid getting into that field (watching porn comes within the gravitational field of adultery).
- Adultery is absolutely prohibited because the Quran wants to protect the institution of the family for the following reasons:
  - It considers the family's unity to be the foundation of society.
  - It gives utmost importance to the welfare of the children in the family, which can only be safeguarded within a healthy family.

Key Points

- It is interesting to note that when the Quran gave the instructions about the etiquette of gender mixing, the first instruction was about "guarding the gazes" because that's the starting point for committing adultery.
- Satan will always suggest that it is OK to be in the field, and you will never get to that act – remember, that's how Satan works.
- Don't overjudge yourself when it comes to the sins that involve sexual behaviors.
- According to the experts:
  - There are five stages of addiction: early exposure, addiction, escalation (something new), desensitization, and acting out sexually.
  - Porn is like a drug on the surface. Cocaine and porn don't seem to have a lot in common, but studies are showing that viewing pornography tricks your brain into releasing the same pleasure chemicals that drugs do.
  - Stats suggest that people who are addicted to watching pornography do not stop watching it even after their marriage, which could be detrimental to the marital relationship (the realities of life often do not match the fantasies shown in such content).
- Recommendations to get rid of this or to avoid this:
  - Find something productive or creative with a higher purpose to keep yourself busy. People usually get involved in this in their free time.
  - Avoid or block all the means that take you towards it.
  - Develop a healthy and loving relationship with your spouse if you are married.
  - Avoid using digital media when you are free. Read a book instead.
  - Keep a good company of friends who are involved in healthy activities like sports, hiking, etc.
  - Repent and make dua to Allah.

Masturbation / Self-Gratification

- One might argue that watching pornography and the act of self-gratification (masturbation) are related, but these are two separate domains as far as religion is concerned; however, studies have found some relationship between the two.

- Also, when examining self-gratification, one should separate its religious and medical/health aspects.

- This is one of those issues faced by almost every member of society, especially when they are growing up and entering adolescence – it is considered a very normal biological urge that is stimulated by the environment they live in.

- In the old days, people used to marry at a very young age, and hence, the topic of self-gratification was not widely discussed. Now, marrying at a younger age is no longer possible due to many social and societal factors.

- In the world of religions, views on self-gratification vary widely – some religions view it as a spiritually detrimental practice and consider it a sin, some see it as not so detrimental, and some see it as acceptable as long as it is used as a means towards sexual self-control, and some see it as acceptable even if there is no reason behind it.

Islam's Position

- The scholars of Islam are divided on its status in Shariah: some consider it prohibited (*Haram*), others consider it disliked (*Makrooh*), and others consider it optional (Mubah).

- It is a fact that no text in the Quran or Ahadith prohibits it – most scholars who consider it prohibited have based their Ijtihad on certain Quranic verses and Ahadith. They use the following verses as evidence:

وَ الَّذِينَ بُمۡ لِفُرُوجِہِمۡ حٰفِظُوۡنَ اِلَّا عَلٰۤی اَزۡوَاجِہِمۡ اَوۡ مَا مَلَکَتۡ اَیۡمَانُہُمۡ فَاِنَّہُمۡ غَیۡرُ مَلُوۡمِیۡنَ

فَمَنِ ابۡتَغٰی وَرَآءَ ذٰلِکَ فَاُولٰٓئِکَ ہُمُ الۡعٰدُوۡنَ

And those who guard their chastity (i.e., private parts), except their wives or the slave girls that their right hands possess. For them, they are free from blame. But whoever seeks beyond that is a transgressor. (Al Muminoon 23:5-7)

Abdullah ibn Masud said, "We were with the Prophet while we were young and had no wealth whatsoever. Allah's Messenger said, 'O young people! Whoever among you can marry should marry because it helps him lower his gaze and guard his private parts, and whoever is not able to marry should fast, as fasting diminishes his sexual power.'" (Al-Bukhari #5066)

- It is obvious that the verse above is alluding to adultery when it calls people "who seek beyond that" transgressors.
- Similarly, the Prophet is advising people in the hadith to stay away from pre-marital sex (Zina).

A weak hadith is also quoted to prove its prohibition: لعن الله ناكح يده

"Allah's curse on the one who is married to his hands"

According to the scholars of Hadith, this is a weak hadith and cannot be presented as evidence.

The Right Approach

- It seems that scholars must take a more pragmatic approach to this in the absence of any clear prohibition.
- After looking at all the religious texts on this topic, it can be easily said that self-gratification cannot be considered Haram, like we consider eating pork or an act of Zina Haram.
- Also, scholars do not consider it wrong if one's spouse performs the same act of gratification for the person, which suggests that the act itself cannot be considered prohibited; in this case, the same act performed by a wife must also be prohibited.
- However, the best that can be said is that it is considered permissible with certain conditions associated with it:
  - It should only be done to release the sexual urge before it gets too powerful for someone to step towards something haram.
  - It should not get converted into an addiction and occupy a person's thoughts all the time.
  - The person must be aware of the health issues associated with it.
  - No external means should be used to incite this urge (for example, watching pornography, or staring at the opposite gender's private parts, etc).
- Here are a few recommendations to keep the urge in check:
  - Set goals and objectives in your life and keep yourself busy working towards them – this will keep you occupied and reduce external stimulation of this internal urge.
  - Follow the beautiful guidance God provided when He spoke about etiquette for meeting people of the opposite gender: "guard your gaze."
  - The objective of attaining Tazkiyah in life must be kept at the center of all our deeds.

Q & A and Discussion

Chapter 18

Islam and Science

This chapter discusses a very important topic that has gained prominence
recently due to some interpreters of the Quran applying new scientific
discoveries to its verses.

Islam and Science

Introduction

Q: If Allah created the laws of science, then why is Islam not compatible with the new scientific discoveries?

"One of the greatest tragedies of our time is this impression that has been created that science and religion have to be at war."
— Francis Collins

DO YOU HAVE TO CHOOSE BETWEEN SCIENCE & RELIGION

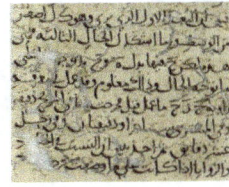

WHAT WOULD YOU SAY?

Astronomical motions Ibn Sina (11th century)

- Many people have faced this situation when talking about religion and/or faith with someone, and the person in turn said, "I don't believe in faith or religion because I believe in science."

- It seems like you can believe in one or the other but not both.

- "Is religion compatible with science?" is the most common question in contemporary discourse.

- Many common Muslims are confused about the relationship between science and religion due to the way the religious circles have responded to the objections raised by the scientific circles on religion.

- Unfortunately, the debate that originated in the Western world in the context of Christianity has somehow been dragged into other faiths, such as Islam.

- This has happened even though during the golden age of Islamic science, which ended somewhere between A.D. 1100 and 1200, Muslim Scientists were way ahead of their contemporaries in Christian Europe, which shows that science is no stranger to Muslims.

- It is also true that some hardcore atheists have brought this discussion into the limelight in recent history to prove their point that people do not need religion or God anymore after science has answered "all" the questions.

- We will see shortly why this entire premise is false.

The domain of Science

- Science is the intellectual and practical activity encompassing the systematic study of the structure and behavior of the physical and natural world through observation and experiment. In simple terms, it is the knowledge of HOW.

- There are many questions in our lives that science has no answer for, and it will never have an answer, even in the future, because the nature of the questions is incompatible with the nature of science.

- Even if science tries to answer any of these questions or similar ones, it will merely be an attempt to disregard religion, but it will have no basis for doing so, nor can it follow scientific methods to prove it.

Questions	Science's Answer
Our purpose in life and on this earth?	X
What is death, and why do we die?	X
What happens to "me" after my death?	X
Where did I get my conscience from?	X
Why is there a universal good and evil?	X
What is sleep and why do I see dreams?	X
Why is there a comprehensive harmony in the universe?	X
Where did this universe come from?	X
Where does mother-child love come from?	X

Why is science mentioned in the Quran?

- The Quran is not a book of science, nor is science its core topic, but it does talk about scientific topics and phenomena.

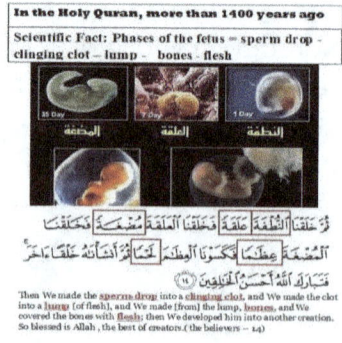

- The Quran is a book of guidance for humanity to know what they need to believe and do to be successful in the life after death – Monotheism, the Day of Judgment, Prophethood, and Life after Death are the main themes of the Quran.
- Nature, natural phenomena, and history are discussed only when God wants to draw people's attention to them in order to present arguments for one of its main themes, such as monotheism.
- The astronomical facts are mentioned in the Quran only to prove the Power, Majesty, and Wisdom of God Almighty.
- Verses related to the beginning of human life and the process of human birth are there only to show that God is the Master Creator, and we should not forget about our insignificance in time.
- However, it is true that if the Quran has discussed a scientific fact while presenting these arguments, then it is not possible for fact-based scientific knowledge to contradict what has been said in the Quran, because the Quran is the book of God, and God created this Universe as well.

The Error in Approaching the Quran

- Human beings create new knowledge, and this knowledge develops over time with no end in sight.
- In every field of science, what humans learned 3000 years ago (philosophy before) did not remain true after 500 years. Similarly, what we learned 500 years ago, a lot of that did not remain true today.
- Modern science (as a result of the Renaissance), which is based solely on observation and experiment, discarded the scientific knowledge (mixed with philosophy) that was purely analogical, deductive, or speculative in the past.
- With this evolving knowledge, the commentators of the Quran used the scientific knowledge of their time to prove the divine nature of the Quran (to explain the verses) without realizing the fact that scientific knowledge evolves, and it will be difficult to justify the explanation of the verses of the Quran when observation and experiment-based scientific knowledge create a completely different world in science.
- Most interpreters of the Quran and scholars have taken this approach in an attempt to answer the question posed at the beginning of this chapter: why the Quran or Islam seems incompatible with modern science. They also wanted to prove the point that the Quran is a miraculous book that was sent 1400+ years ago, containing this scientific knowledge.

How to Approach the Quran

- When interpreting the Quran, translators and interpreters must not go beyond its general principles, even when interpreting verses related to science. The general principles of understanding the text of the Quran are:
    - Look at the word used in the verse in the light of the classical Arabic of the time of the revelation of the Quran.
    - Determine the shade of the word that is used due to the way the sentence was constructed.
    - The limitations and boundaries that the word needs to take are due to the context in which the verse is coming.
- The verses of the Quran must NOT be interpreted in the light of the knowledge of that time. However, there is no harm in mentioning the scientific discoveries while explaining the verses, but the interpretation of the verses must not be based on scientific knowledge.

Issues in approaching the Quran via Science

Do those who have disbelieved see/realize that the Heavens and the Earth were joined together and We clove them asunder (separated them via the Big Bang)? (21:30)

- What's presented above is the most common translation done by the recent translators of the Quran.
- Some physicists question what existed before the Big Bang and whether the concept of a singularity (a point of infinite density and temperature) accurately describes the universe's origin (as interpreted from the verse).
- Some critics of the Big Bang theory say it violates the first law of thermodynamics, which states that matter and energy cannot be created or destroyed. Critics claim that the Big Bang theory suggests the universe began from nothing, which is unscientific.
- However, the "debate" is less about replacing the theory and more about refining it, driven by inconsistencies between predictions and observations.

How would we interpret this verse if, after 100 years, the scientific community changed its position on the Big Bang due to newer discoveries?

Theory of Evolution

  ?

Many influential groups of society have tried to hijack the theory of evolution to support all kinds of man-made ideologies – atheism, racism, communism, capitalism ......

- The theory of evolution aims to explain the origins and phenomena of biological diversity – it has nothing to do with philosophy.
- If science can describe the mechanism behind the evolution of life, it does not, in itself, undermine the Creator.
- Scientists are collecting material evidence in the form of fossils to support the theory.
- The reason it appears to conflict with Islam is how the scholars of Islam have tried to explain the origin of the human race – the most popular explanation is that God asked angels to bring soil from 4 different continents, which He used to make a human sculpture and blew His Spirit in it, which formed the first human being, Adam.
- This story does not exist in the Quran.
- However, a deeper study of the verses of the Quran on this topic suggests that the Quran's idea about the origin of human life is quite close to what the theory of evolution is trying to present for micro-evolution, keeping in mind that this is not the topic of the Quran, but God has alluded to the origin of mankind in several verses.
- The Quran does not allude to macroevolution and actually stands against it.

And He is the One who created everything to its perfection, and He **started the creation of humans from clay**. **Then He continued** his generation from the extract of an insignificant fluid. (Surah Sajdah: 8-9)

Quran and Origin of Life

- There are other verses in the Quran that do address the origin of life, but they only offer hints that scientific communities should investigate further, as this is not the Quran's topic.

فَاسْتَفْتِهِمْ اَهُمْ اَشَدُّ خَلْقًا اَمْ مَّنْ خَلَقْنَا إِنَّا خَلَقْنٰهُمْ مِّنْ طِينٍ لَّازِبٍ

So, ask them if creating them is more difficult than what We have created before (Jinns and Angels). Indeed, We created them (humans) from sticky clay. (Surah Saffaat:11)

وَ لَقَدْ خَلَقْنَا الْاِنْسَانَ مِنْ سُلٰلَةٍ مِّنْ طِينٍ ثُمَّ جَعَلْنٰهُ نُطْفَةً فِيْ قَرَارٍ مَّكِيْنٍ

And certainly, We created humans from an extract of clay. Then We placed him as a semen drop in a firm lodging. (Surah Muminoon: 12-13)

وَ اللهُ اَنْبَتَكُمْ مِّنَ الْاَرْضِ نَبَاتًا

And Allah has grown you from the earth in a special way. (Surah Nuh: 17)

Key Points

- The Quran suggests that the process of human creation began in the soil near a beach or a body of water, which is sticky (clay).

- This process was similar to the one that occurs inside a mother's womb at a micro level, when sperm and egg combine (extract from food with the same ingredients as the earth).

- Then humans were given the ability to procreate.

- After a long time, God selected two from among many within the human species and honored them with His blow, which created the human 'personality,' including the intellect in us.

- Evolution is all around us. For example, the various types of delicious vegetables we eat today have come from a few wild ancestors that farmers selected from hundreds of varieties.

Evolution in Plants

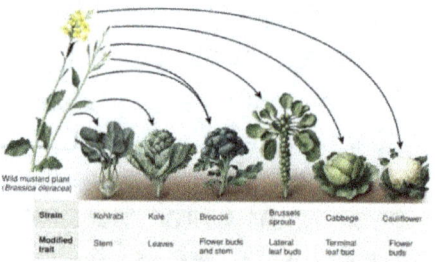

Islamic scholars who talked about some type of Evolution in nature:
- Al Jaheth (776-868)
- Ibn Miskawayh (932-1030)
- Ikhwan as Safa (10th century)
- Ibn Khaldun (14th century)
- Al Jisr (1880s)
- Ahmad Midhat (1880s)

- The fact that randomness and variation among species, and the process of adaptation, play a role in their survival is quite visible and cannot be denied at the microlevel.
- From the Islamic point of view, God created everything, including the process of evolution and natural selection within the species – this is like, for example, the laws of physics that govern various phenomena in this universe or our birth process in a mother's womb that lasts for around nine months. Every creation goes through a process.

Theory of evolution is hijacked

Last paragraph from Charles Darwin's book Origin of Species

from the indirect and direct action of the external conditions of life, and from use and disuse; a Ratio of Increase so high as to lead to a Struggle for Life, and as a consequence to Natural Selection, entailing Divergence of Character and the Extinction of less-improved forms. Thus, from the war of nature, from famine and death, the most exalted object which we are capable of conceiving, namely, the production of the higher animals, directly follows.   There is grandeur in this view of life, with its several powers, having been originally breathed by the Creator into a few forms or into one; and that, whilst this planet has gone cycling on according to the fixed law of gravity, from so simple a beginning endless forms most beautiful and most wonderful have been, and are being, evolved.

- Richard Dawkins famously stated in his book that "Darwin made it possible to be an 'intellectually fulfilled atheist' by providing a naturalistic explanation for the complexity of life, thereby eliminating the need for a creator."
- It is quite clear that Darwinism is a scientific theory designed to explain biological diversity, which has been wrongly elevated by some into a comprehensive philosophy (scientism) to disprove God, a move not inherent in the scientific theory itself.
- Charles Darwin described himself as an agnostic rather than an atheist, and he famously resisted attempts to drag his scientific work into militant atheistic activism during his lifetime.
- Darwin presented the theory of evolution by natural selection to explain the origin of species and biological complexity, not primarily to answer theological or philosophical questions, though his work certainly challenged traditional theological views of design.

Q & A and Discussion

Chapter 19

Islam and Atheism

This chapter discusses a very important topic that has gained prominence recently due to the growth of militant atheists who are pushing hard against any form of religion, not just Islam.

Islam and Atheism

Definition of Atheism (as they say it)

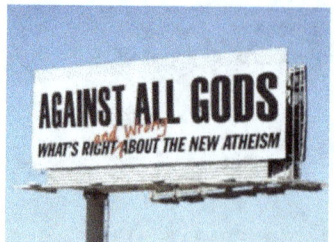 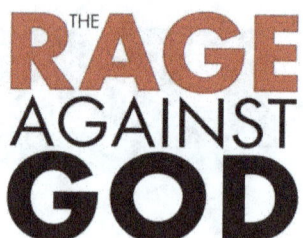

Atheism is <u>not</u> disbelief in gods or a denial of their existence; it is a lack of belief in them. (American Atheists)

- Sometimes researchers group atheists, agnostics, humanists, freethinkers, unaffiliated/nones into atheists category.
- Some people do not believe in a god but still do not call themselves atheists – technically, they are atheists, but they do not insist (in reality, they are agnostics).
- A recent survey from University of Kentucky psychologists Will Gervais and Maxine Najle found that as many as 26% of Americans may be atheists ("maybe" indicates that all sorts of people are included in this survey).
- The actual number of 'convinced atheists' is way smaller than what appears in the surveys.

Is Atheism really growing fast?

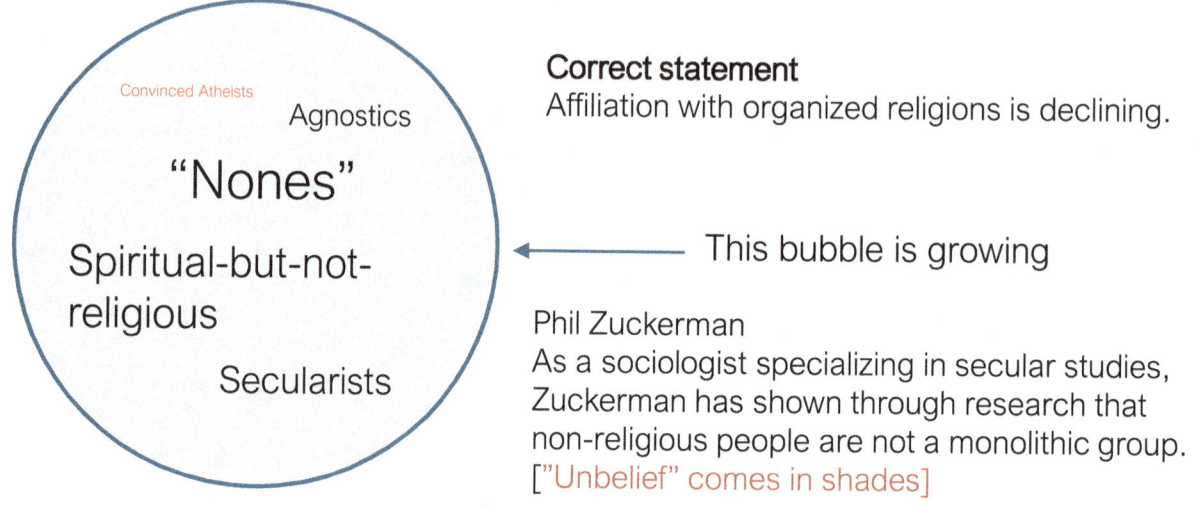

Convinced Atheists

Agnostics

"Nones"

Spiritual-but-not-religious

Secularists

Correct statement
Affiliation with organized religions is declining.

This bubble is growing

Phil Zuckerman
As a sociologist specializing in secular studies, Zuckerman has shown through research that non-religious people are not a monolithic group. ["Unbelief" comes in shades]

Growing disassociation with organized religion & our reaction

- As seen before, the number of atheists is growing in the world, but there is a larger group of people who call themselves agnostics, naturalists, and unaffiliated because they are not sure "if there is a God".

- Sometimes, agnostics or unaffiliated also call themselves "spiritual but not religious".

- Anti-theists, a very small group of activists, argue that believing in a God harms the person, society, politics, culture, etc. They also think theists should be confronted to reduce the harm caused by believing in theism.

- This group has given birth to "new atheism," which in itself is turning into a religion – the arguments presented by the "new atheists" like Sam Harris, Richard Dawkins, and Christopher Hitchens are often just as violent as those presented by some of the religious groups.

- As expected, the reaction of Muslims towards this group is abusive, violent, and immoral, which is not only unhelpful but also causes more people to leave Islam as a result of this attitude.

Reasons for growing atheism

- A large population of common people who are not very religious is getting intimidated by the behavior and attitude of religious people, especially leaders of organized religions like Islam and Christianity.

- Violence committed by so-called religious groups in the name of religion has forced people to think that religion somehow promotes violence, which is completely against their concept of religion.

- Religious people have tried to solve the problems of the world through religion, which religion never came to solve in the first place, and their proposed solution is not implementable in the 21st century.

- Traditionally trained religious scholars are unable to satisfactorily answer the difficult questions raised by intellectuals, especially by the younger generation.

- "Freedom," as a value, has gained importance in the lives of common people, and they want the freedom to choose their lifestyle, which is more relevant and appealing.

- People who are intellectuals and influenced by science argue that because everything in this universe can be explained by science without involving God, then there is no 'need' for God – they are hopeful that the questions that science is unable to answer today will be able to answer tomorrow – on the other hand, religious people have given an impression to the world that they are anti-science.

- Most of the people who drifted towards atheism argue that if God is All-Good, All-Knowing, All-Powerful, and All-Merciful, then why is the world full of evil and wickedness?

Main arguments of Atheism

General argument: "Atheists don't have to give any arguments on atheism because the burden of proof is on the one who believes in something positively".

Specific arguments (explanation of their position) Source: American Atheists

1. There is inadequate scientific evidence for God's existence – there is no persuasive "reason" to believe in God.

2. An all-good and all-powerful God and pain/suffering/injustice cannot coexist – also called the problem of evil.

3. There are so many "versions" of God; all cannot be true at the same time.

4. There is incoherence in many religious concepts, such as free will and an all-knowing God.

5. As the natural sciences advance and explain phenomena, they diminish the need for the supernatural.

6. Historical "evidence" suggests that any belief in God emerged from the psychological and sociological factors/needs of human beings, natural forces, finding comfort, etc.

Analysis of the Arguments

The Argument of Scientific Evidence

- Science, based on observations, is just one source of knowledge. God is outside the physical universe, so direct observation of Him is impossible.

- On the other hand, inference is a fundamental aspect of scientific reasoning, enabling scientists to move from raw data and observations to meaningful conclusions that advance our understanding of the world. Examples:
  - **Observation:** The coastlines of South America and Africa fit together like pieces of a puzzle.
  - **Reliable Inference:** These continents were once connected as part of a supercontinent.
  - **Observation:** Global temperatures have been rising over the past century.
  - **Reliable Inference:** Human activities, such as the burning of fossil fuels, are contributing to the increase in greenhouse gases in the atmosphere.

- Science lacks answers to many realities of this world that are as real as physical things – morals, persona, why things happen in a certain way, our conscience, innate knowledge of good and evil, etc.

The problem of evil

- Life is created as a test because of the free will granted to us by God. If God intervenes, the grand scheme of the test will fail.
- The so-called evil in the form of natural phenomena like disasters or death is not evil in the complete picture of this universe. It all ends up well in the sight of God.
- The evil committed by human beings is simply the exercise of free will, which God allows for a limited time. He sometimes intervenes if it is required in the grand scheme of things.

Versions of God

- God's religion has always been Islam since the time of the first human being. It is humans who corrupted the message and introduced innovation in God's religion.
- That's why the world religions, in general, share a lot, because they all started with the true religion of God.

Incoherence in religion

- The seemingly incoherent concepts can be easily understood in the light of the grand scheme God presented in the Quran.
- Life in this world and life in the Hereafter together complete the full picture; neither should be viewed in isolation.
- The seemingly contradictory attributes of God, such as Justice and Mercy existing simultaneously, seem inconsistent to us because we see God through a human perspective. He is God, not a human.

The development of natural sciences

- The development of natural sciences only explains the phenomena behind natural processes. It does not negate the existence of God, who designed the natural processes in such a way.
- God explained in the Quran that He continually creates things step by step, progressing toward completion. A child in a mother's womb goes through a 9-month cycle to completion.

Historical "evidence"

- Written human history dates back only 5-6 thousand years. However, humans' actual history can be traced back millions of years. We cannot infer the origins of the concept of God simply by looking at 5,000 years of history. According to the history described in the Quran, humans started their journey on this earth with one God.

Quran on Atheism

- The Quran does not deal with the issue of atheism directly because the recognition of an Almighty is innate in human nature.

- The incident of the Pledge (see below Aaraf 172), as the Quran puts it, caused this recognition to be stamped on the human heart and ingrained in the soul (becoming a common heritage of humankind) – the incident is erased from memory, for this life to be a trial.

- Also, everything within us and in the external world strongly suggests that it was created carefully and meticulously, leading us to one of the most basic questions that every one of us has in mind: "Who is our Creator?"

- The concept of God is so innate and complies with our intuition and common sense that we all feel inclined to embrace it without hesitation, answering a natural need.

- So, whether they admit it or not, Atheists also believe in a Creator, but they believe that this universe has all the ingredients to create itself. There is no denying the fact that we and everything around us are created.

- So, the real debate about Creator is:

The universe has a Creator	OR	The universe is the Creator

اَمْ خُلِقُوا مِنْ غَيْرِ شَيْءٍ اَمْ هُمُ الْخٰلِقُوْنَ ۞ اَمْ خَلَقُوا السَّمٰوٰتِ وَ الْاَرْضَ ۚ بَلْ لَّا يُوْقِنُوْنَ

Have they come into existence without any creator? Or are they their creators? Or have they created the heavens and the earth? Nay, they are not certain [for they are blinded by doubt]! (Surah Tur:35-36)

Note: *Some scholars present these verses in response to Atheism, but these questions were put to Polytheists in Makkah who believed in God but denied the Hereafter. The Quran argued that the Day of Judgment is the necessary consequence of a Just Creator.*

وَ اِذْ اَخَذَ رَبُّكَ مِنْ بَنِيْ اٰدَمَ مِنْ ظُهُوْرِهِمْ ذُرِّيَّتَهُمْ وَ اَشْهَدَهُمْ عَلٰى اَنْفُسِهِمْ اَلَسْتُ بِرَبِّكُمْ ۚ قَالُوْا بَلٰى ۚ شَهِدْنَا ۚ اَنْ تَقُوْلُوْا يَوْمَ الْقِيٰمَةِ اِنَّا كُنَّا عَنْ هٰذَا غٰفِلِيْنَ

And (remind them) when your Lord took out from the children of Adam, from their loins, their descendants, and made them bear witness against their souls: (He asked) 'Am I not your Lord?' All unequivocally replied, 'Verily, you are! We bear witness to this", (and this is done) so that they would not say on the Day of Judgment, "indeed, we were not even aware of this" (Surah Aaraf:172)

The Evidence of God

- There is multiple evidence for God. When looking at the matter, all evidence must be considered together, as it supports one another and points to God.
- The picture below shows all the evidence, from our intuition to the physical evidence in the form of destruction of nations preserved for us in the Quran, which has happened multiple times, including the last time 1400 years ago.

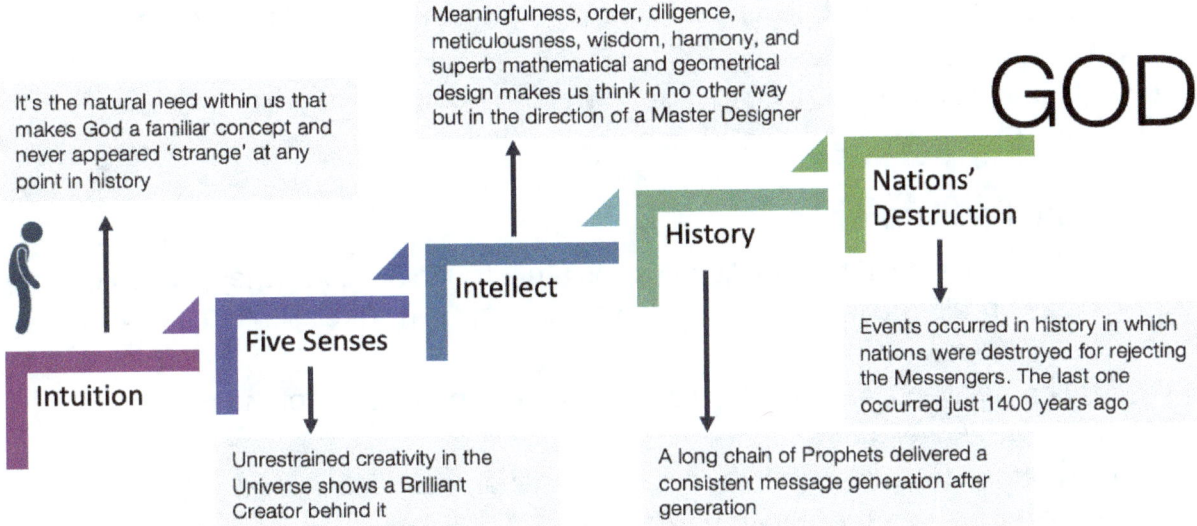

- **Intuition:** Humans have an inherent, natural need for a creator, making the concept of God feel familiar and persistent throughout history.
- **Five Senses:** The immense creativity, intricate complexity, and ongoing harmony observed in the universe through our senses suggest the presence of a "Brilliant Creator."
- **Intellect:** The mathematical order, harmony, and design found in nature intellectually lead one to believe in a "Master Designer."
- **History:** A "long chain of Prophets" who have consistently delivered the same message about God across different generations. Their account has been recorded in many religious books, including the Quran.
- **Nations' destruction:** These are historical events in which civilizations were destroyed for rejecting messengers, with a particular event from 1,400 years ago recorded in the Quran as evidence of divine punishment. The leaders of Quraysh were all killed at the hands of Muslims (with the help of angels) in the famous Battle of Badr, despite the fact that Muslims were 1/3rd of the enemy army in number.

Other groups

"I am spiritual but not religious" group

The concept behind it

- A growing number of people claim they are "good people" or "spiritual" people, but do not believe in any 'organized religion' or at least not practicing the religion they originally associated with.
- They think that organized religions instituted by God cause more harm than good.
- People from all religious backgrounds, including Christians/Muslims, are joining this group.
- Everyone is "spiritual" or "good" in their own terms, with the meaning only they understand.

Root of the Problem

- 'Religious people' tried to 'solve' every problem through religion – they presented religion as an 'alternative' to fix the world's problems, which religion did not come for in the first place.
- They became averse to the rude, violent, and corrupt behavior of the religious leaders and their followers.
- The "Freedom" to choose a lifestyle is more relevant, appealing, and "cool".
- It is much easier to be "spiritual" than "religious" as religion puts so many boundaries.

Dangers of areligious life

- Areligious life is a reaction, not a thoughtful conclusion.
- This leads to complacency and self-centeredness.
- There are no common societal aims or goals.
- Being "good" is subjective and can lead to egotism.
- Truth and God's Will become irrelevant because of lost objectivity.
- In essence, it is "piggybacking" on religious goodness (from human history) without carrying religion's baggage.
- In this case, a sense of accountability before God is seriously lacking.
- People can blend Buddhism, Taoism, Judaism, Sufism, and other beliefs to "make" a belief system of their own. "Everything" is good.
- Unknowingly connotate that God is 'irresponsible' and never communicates to us after creating us.

Few Key Points

- Atheism has existed in this world in one form or another since Greek Philosophy was at its peak (5th Century BC). However, the first people to identify themselves as atheists lived in the 18th century, during the Age of Enlightenment.
- One of the main reasons behind the popularity of atheism is that the intellectuals and religious scholars did not make any arrangements to educate the masses about religion. Most people learn it from the environment they are born in, without getting any proper education about it.
- Growing atheism in the Islamic world and among Muslims is a reaction to the atrocities, corruption, and the inability to answer people's difficult questions by the religious elites who are not trained to meet the intellectual challenges of the 21st century.
- Many former Muslims who have become atheists express frustration with the state of affairs within the Muslim community, particularly in religious circles. They find it difficult to believe that God would create such a religion.

How to approach a new ideology?

- One must learn the methodology for understanding any ideology presented. For example, Muslims should never stay as "born Muslims" their whole life, but instead, at some point, must take the journey of becoming a "conscious Muslim or Muslim by choice."
- Try to grasp the rationale behind any proposition or argument and understand the foundation on which the results have been drawn while resisting the captivating effects of the manner in which it has been presented.
- Test that proposition on the following basis for reasoning: physical observation, human experience, the historical account of human beings' collective observation and experiences, and rational inference (logical deductions) from what can be observed.
- Learn how to scrutinize the foundational reasoning of any ideology on the above criteria before accepting any influence from it.

Q & A and Discussion

Chapter 20

Human Rights and Islam

This chapter discusses a very important topic that has gained prominence in the last century and that is human rights. In this chapter we will explore the areas of compatibility and apparent conflict between Islam and Universal Declaration of Human Rights by United Nations.

Background

Introduction

- The UN adopted the Universal Declaration of Human Rights (UDHR) in 1948, signed by many Muslim countries.
- It was shaped by various historical and philosophical sources:
  - Legal and historical precedents like Magna Carta, the French Declaration of the Rights of Man and of the Citizen, the US Bill of Rights
  - World War II Atrocities
  - Philosophical traditions like secular enlightenment ideas
  - Franklin D. Roosevelt's 1941 speech on the Four Freedoms (Freedom of Speech, Freedom of Religion, Freedom from Want, and Freedom from Fear)

- Islamic teachings and HR law share overlapping concerns, prompting comparison.
- Some aspects of HR law are consistent with Islamic teachings (re-introduced in the 6th century), and some are not.
- We will look into the extent of cooperation possible with inconsistent aspects and the reasons behind them.

"Huquq ul Ibaad"

- Within Islamic theology, human rights have existed since the birth of humanity with Adam, as they are inherent privileges granted by God. That's why from Islamic perspective, the concept of human rights did not begin as a new philosophical idea in the 6th century. Instead, it is viewed as a restoration and codification of rights that God granted to humanity at the moment of creation.
- In the Quranic framework, "human rights" are always framed as "*Huquq ul Ibaad*" (the rights of the servants of God). Since these rights are given by God, they are viewed as immutable obligations. For example, a person's life, wealth and honor must be protected in Islam and no one should violate them.

Islam and Human Rights

Divine revelation and collective human wisdom

- According to the Quranic understanding, collective human wisdom—rooted in human nature—is not in conflict with Divine Revelation as presented in the Quran. However, humans face two crucial challenges:
- We cannot always reach definitive answers to certain issues on our own.
- Human intellect can be degraded by prolonged exposure to adverse environments or deliberate indulgence in known vices.
- The Quran boldly asserts that a sound human intellect would inevitably align with Divine Revelation. This is why it intentionally limits itself to addressing only a few areas for regulating individual and communal Muslim life.
- Such an approach leaves ample room for harmony between Islamic teachings and secular understandings of human-related rules.

فَاَقِمْ وَجْهَكَ لِلدِّيْنِ حَنِيْفًا ۚ فِطْرَتَ اللّٰهِ الَّتِيْ فَطَرَ النَّاسَ عَلَيْهَا ۚ لَا تَبْدِيْلَ لِخَلْقِ اللّٰهِ ۚ ذٰلِكَ الدِّيْنُ الْقَيِّمُ ۙ وَ لٰكِنَّ اَكْثَرَ النَّاسِ لَا يَعْلَمُوْنَ

So, [now that these facts have become evident,] following one God, continue to point your face [like your father Ibrahim] towards his religion (religion of Ibrahim). [O Prophet] Follow the nature created by God on which He has created people [this religion complies fully with your nature]. This nature created by God cannot be changed. This is the only straight path, but most people do not know it. (Surah Rum: 30)

Human Rights in Islam – Agreement

1. Islam considers the sanctity of human life, property, and honor to be absolute. For example, it states that killing one innocent person is akin to killing all humanity, and unjustly seizing another's wealth is strictly forbidden; protecting a person's reputation is a religious duty with punishments declared for those who violate it (*Qadhf*).
2. The rights of parents, children, minorities, prisoners, spouses, and the poor are recognized. For example, Zakah is a mandatory charity, and minorities were guaranteed protection of their faith and property.

3. Elimination of slavery (verses of Surah Muhammad revealed before the first major fight and many other steps taken by the Quran), and humane treatment of POWs (aligned with the Geneva Convention).
4. Freedom of thought and expression. No compulsion in religion, the Quran declared.
5. Consultative governance (*Shoora is recommended in the Quran*) is consistent with democratic principles.

Misunderstood Issues – Non-issues

Minority(*) Rights

- Islam guarantees equal rights to worship, employment, and religious practice (Hijaz may be an exception due to the overall scheme of God as explained in the Quran and by Prophet Muhammad).

- Christian missionaries have operated in Muslim countries for centuries, often unnoticed by the state, and have regularly converted Muslims to Christianity despite Islamic teachings condemning apostasy.

- In some Muslim countries, such as Pakistan, the rule that the head of state must be Muslim is based on their laws, even though it is not directly prescribed by Islamic teachings.

Slavery

- Islam's teachings aimed to eliminate slavery completely. However, the Quran addressed the issue gradually to avoid harm, not through a single command, which was not properly understood and practiced, even by Muslims.

- There is a series of instructions meant to uplift the status of slaves on the one hand and pave the way for their permanent emancipation on the other, if the slaves are in a position to do so.

* This debate is not relevant to current nation-states formed after WWII, as in such states, the idea of a minority pertains to the democratic processes of electing officials and forming governments, and is not related to religious identity.

Democratic culture

- It is often misrepresented that Islam does not view democracy or democratic culture favorably.
- The understanding is partly shaped by the perception of predominantly dictatorial monarchies detailed in the history of Muslim dynasties and partly by the impression of contemporary Muslim states, where genuine democracies are scarcely visible in over fifty countries.
- Islam's teachings when Muslims gain the majority and form a government:
  - Decision-making, including the formation of the government, should involve mutual consultation among participants (citizens of the state).
  - The political system and governance should align with Islamic teachings.
  - The public should obey their rulers.

Democracy Index, 2024-25

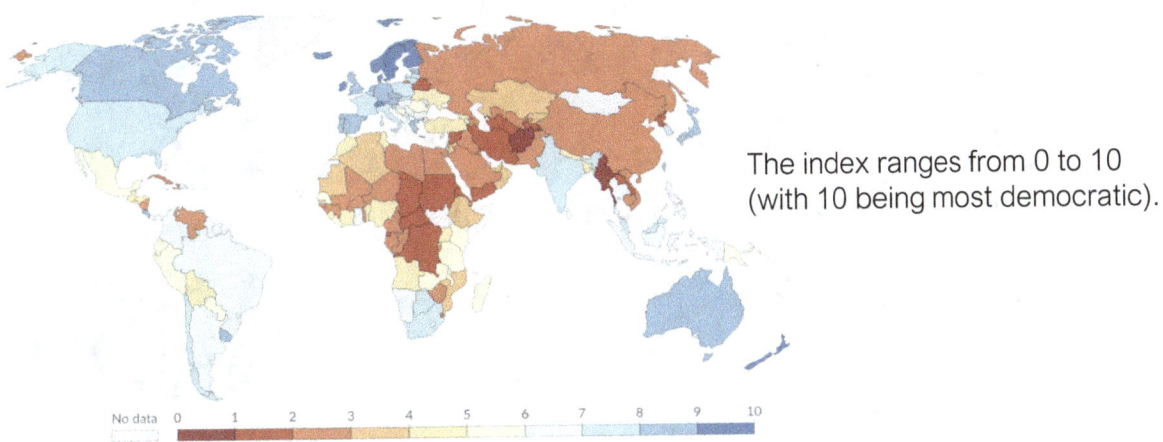

The index ranges from 0 to 10 (with 10 being most democratic).

Jihad (most misunderstood)

- Many believe that Muslims are justified by their religion to fight with other nations if they find a religious excuse.
- This view has strengthened due to some Muslim groups' aggressive actions and negative media campaigns aimed at tarnishing Islam's image.
- This is caused by a misunderstanding of some of the laws mentioned in the Quran:
  - There is a divine punishment inflicted by God on those who deliberately rejected His message through His messenger Muhammad, often through military aggression, unlike earlier prophets like Noah and Moses, where punishments came through natural calamities.
  - The Islamic law prohibits creating chaos and mischief on earth; such individuals or groups should be either mercilessly killed or banished.

- On the other hand, in the Quran, killing a single innocent soul without just cause is seen as equivalent to killing all of mankind; saving a single life is regarded as as virtuous as saving all of humanity.
- In Shariah, lifting weapons of war is only justified under a legitimate ruler's command for a just cause, primarily to eliminate oppression and injustice, and not for military adventurism or guerrilla warfare.

Areas of Disagreement

1. Corporal and capital punishments prescribed in Shariah conflict with HR norms on bodily integrity.
2. Gender-differentiated rules on divorce, inheritance, dress, and marital authority conflict with equality principles.

The System of Criminal Punishments

- The Quran mandates a strict justice system for Muslims:
    - Executing murderers and those guilty of creating mischief on earth
    - Publicly flogging adulterers and fornicators with a hundred lashes
    - Punishing false accusers of chaste individuals with eighty lashes
    - Amputating the hand of a thief
- Human rights activists see these punishments as violating fundamental human rights.

Ideological Difference between Islam and Secular Worldview

- In **Islam**, the life is a creation of an all-wise, all-knowing God, designed to give humans the opportunity to live morally responsible lives.
- This earthly existence is a temporary trial, leading to accountability and eternal rewards or punishments.
- Humans are guided by their God-given nature and intellect, as well as by divine revelation through prophets, in our case, with the Quran and the Prophet's Sunnah, which helps them realize their moral potential despite their limitations.
- An ideal Islamic society fosters an environment in which individuals can achieve their goals. Punishment, whether capital or physical, offers offenders a chance to repent and improve their prospects in the afterlife.

- The **secular worldview** regards questions about the Creator and the purpose of creation as unimportant (or almost irrelevant).
- According to the common view among secular thinkers, alongside physical evolution, there is also ongoing moral and intellectual development in humans.
- Humans have won the conflict between religious beliefs and Enlightenment ideas.
- It is now widely accepted that although religion played a role in an early stage of human social development, it is now a thing of the past, only fit to be kept in a museum as part of mankind's history of spiritual and intellectual struggles.
- The human rights ideology would strongly oppose inflicting physical pain on an individual, considering that this life is the only opportunity for human existence.

Gender Differences in Various Laws

- **Islam** emphasizes strengthening the family, reducing extramarital sex, and discouraging unnecessary attraction to the opposite sex to support spiritual growth (same goal as before).
- The family structure, inheritance laws, and other rules are established so that men and women collaborate as partners, based on their moral, spiritual, intellectual, and creative abilities, rather than as rivals.
- Islam has contributed to improving women's status, raising them from a 'thing' to a more dignified position.

Note: *All subject laws are given with the provision that if and when circumstances change, new laws can be derived to support the new situation (For example, Nikah is an agreement between two parties, and there is a provision of Will under inheritance laws)*

- **Philosophers of human rights** see history as a progression from a patriarchal society where women were treated as inferior or non-human.
- However, Islam's role as a bridge from the Dark Ages to enlightenment has fulfilled its purpose, and its utility in advancing gender equality is considered outdated.
- Women now deserve equal rights with men in all areas of life, aside from biological differences given by nature.
- Human progress in moral and social development has reached a high point, and setbacks are seen as inappropriate and should be rejected.

Conclusion

- There is a broad area of human affairs where human rights and Islamic teachings align.

- The Islamic rationale for this compatibility is that divine revelation, which forms the basis of Islamic teachings, recognizes the value of human intellect and regards it as sacred. Human intellect is a gift from God, so it can often arrive at correct or nearly correct conclusions.

- However, it is important to appreciate why there are both agreements and disagreements between these two views on practical matters. It's good to realize that, despite their differences, the practical gaps are not as large as one might think.

- However, when it comes to their fundamental worldviews, the gap is very wide. These views are completely opposite, and reconciliation is not possible in this area.

- What's important is to avoid arrogance and disrespect when exchanging ideas.

- Influential people or groups should not dismiss the other view as useless or unworthy. Likewise, no one should try to force their beliefs onto others.

The fundamental philosophical difference between the two systems can only be resolved through peaceful debate, a struggle that has persisted since humanity's intellectual origins. These conflicts will continue into the future, with victories and defeats. Our hope—and we must work to realize it—is that this debate occurs in intellectual venues such as bookstores, libraries, conferences, and the media, rather than in war zones, training camps, or 'closed-door' strategic meetings.

Q & A and Discussion

Chapter 21

Various Topics

This chapter discusses Islam's position on various topics that are listed on the next page.

Topics Covered

Is Cloning allowed in Islam?

Can I donate my organs?

Are sex-change operations permissible?

Is cosmetic surgery allowed in Islam?

What is the position of Islam on assisted suicide?

A – Is cloning allowed in Islam?

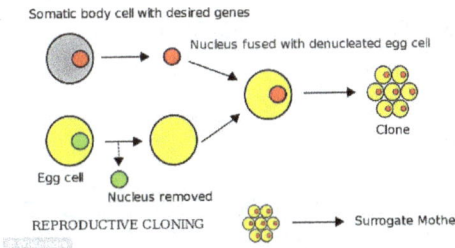

Somatic body cell with desired genes

Nucleus fused with denucleated egg cell

Clone

Egg cell

Nucleus removed

REPRODUCTIVE CLONING → Surrogate Mother

Cloning describes the processes used to create an exact genetic replica of another cell, tissue, or organism. The copied material, which has the same genetic makeup as the original, is called a clone. The most famous clone was a Scottish sheep named Dolly. (US National Library of Medicine)

- A few decades ago, cloning was science fiction, but recent scientific and technological advances have made it a real possibility.
- Because of the risks and complications associated with reproductive cloning, the process faces ethical objections from almost all segments of society – there are a lot of questions raised about the psychology of the "product" itself.
- Like in almost all cases, Islam does not interfere with scientific research and discoveries unless it has ethical or moral implications, especially if they are related to human beings.
- Several questions can be raised that may have ethical implications:
  - Will this new' copy' introduce any physiological or psychological complications?
  - What would be the status of these 'beings' in society?
  - If, due to some complications, a defective being is produced, then what would be the ruling for such a person, and who will be held responsible for the sufferings of that 'person'?

B – Can I donate my organs?

- Shariah is quiet about the question of organ donation because it has only come in recent times due to the advancements in science.

- Although there is a difference of opinion among scholars, and a minority views it as a desecration of the body (something against the dignity of a deceased Muslim), more and more Muslims believe its benefits outweigh the concerns raised by a few.

- If no moral or ethical questions are raised about organ donation, then it should be praised, encouraged, and considered an act of continuous charity (Sadaqah e Jariyah).

- When people go out to war, they often sacrifice their limbs and their bodies for the sake of God – this is also for the betterment of ill fellow human beings whose lives could be transformed after they receive the organ.

- The spirit of charity must be maintained when agreeing to the donation.

- Even though one has the right to do it, putting certain conditions and preferences about who it should be donated to (for example, Muslims vs non-Muslims) should be avoided, and let the medical institute decide based on the need and circumstances.

C – Are sex-change operations permissible?

- The term "transgender" refers to a person whose sex assigned at birth does not match their gender identity (the inner feeling of the gender) – some of them experience what is called "gender dysphoria" (psychological distress).

- In such situations, transgender people may pursue gender affirmation (or reassignment) through a surgery called surgical affirmation.

- If the matter is related to a situation where it is medically possible to reassign gender later in life through reassignment surgery, then it is allowed; however, it is prohibited to go through such a medical procedure if it's undertaken because someone wants to do it.

- If a person goes through such an operation just because he/she wants to have a different gender, then that would be considered "changing the creation of Allah," which is considered an abhorrent act in the Quran (4:119 and 30:30).

- It should be looked at as a biological disorder, and the person has the right to seek medical help for both biological and psychological treatments.

D – Is cosmetic surgery allowed in Islam?

- Cosmetic surgery can be done for two purposes:
  - For fixing a birth defect or an injury caused by an accident, it is definitely permissible.
  - For beautification – it is also allowed, and the ruling is similar to makeup, which is left to the aesthetic sense of the person (some scholars put it in the category of "not encouraged" because people often go towards extremes and change themselves to a degree where it is hard to recognize the original person).
- Also, sometimes cosmetic surgery could be used to deceive other people by artificially beautifying oneself, which is definitely prohibited – an example would be when an older woman goes through plastic surgery to look younger.
- If the purpose is to look better, for example, a grown adult dying his/her hair, it is allowed.

E – What is the position of Islam on Assisted Suicide?

Euthanasia and physician-assisted suicide refer to deliberate actions taken with the intention of ending a life in order to relieve persistent suffering.

- This life is a test, and God has kept the matters of life and death in His own Hands and does not allow anyone to take this matter into their own hands.
- For a believer, life does not end with death, but it is the beginning of another life whose pleasures and agony will depend entirely on how we perform in this test.
- The suffering that a person is going through is part of the test, and God will compensate for the patience that a person displays in such circumstances in the form of a great reward on the Day of Judgment.
- The best we can do is to continue to look for the cure and leave the results with God.
- If a person or his/her family decides to remove life-support equipment because it was keeping his/her alive artificially (with no hope for improvement), then there is no harm in that, but requesting assisted suicide is completely prohibited in Islam.

"Nothing afflicts a Muslim of hardship, illness, anxiety, sorrow, harm, distress, or even the pricking of a thorn, but that Allah will expiate his sins by it." (Sahih Al Bukhari #5641)

"Verily, Allah Almighty will put His servant to trial by illness until his every sin is expiated." (Al Mujam al Kabir #1548)

Q & A and Discussion

www.ingramcontent.com/pod-product-compliance
Lightning Source LLC
Chambersburg PA
CBHW081327120626

46546CB00011B/3258